Leesylvania Elementary School
15800 Neabsco Road
Woodbridge, VA 22191

PREPARING STUDENTS TO RAISE ACHIEVEMENT SCORES

Grades 3–4

by Darriel Ledbetter and
Leland Graham

Incentive Publications, Inc.
Nashville, Tennessee

The authors of this book would like to gratefully acknowledge
the assistance and suggestions of the following persons:

Virginia Brickman, Stan Carey, Brenda Colburn,
Harriett Cook, Dan Gasparrini and Instructional Informatics, Inc.,
Sue Godbey, Chris Higgins, Robert Kingsbury, Brenda Langseth,
Frankie Long, Chris McClellan, Melissa McClendon, Beverly Moody,
David Park, Laura Sharp, and Nancy Zwald.

Illustrated by Kathleen Bullock
Cover by Marta Drayton & Joe Shibley

ISBN 0-86530-332-0

Copyright ©1996 by Incentive Publications, Inc., Nashville, TN. All rights reserved. No part of this publication may be reproduced, stored in a retrieval system, or transmitted in any form or by any means (electronic, mechanical, photocopying, recording, or otherwise) without written permission from Incentive Publications, Inc., with the exception below.

Pages labeled with the statement **©1996 by Incentive Publications, Inc., Nashville, TN** are intended for reproduction. Permission is hereby granted to the purchaser of one copy of PREPARING STUDENTS TO RAISE ACHIEVEMENT SCORES, GRADES 3–4 to reproduce these pages in sufficient quantities for meeting the purchaser's own classroom needs.

PRINTED IN THE UNITED STATES OF AMERICA

Table of Contents

INTRODUCTION vi

CHAPTER ONE 7–11
    Teaching Test-Taking and Study Skills

CHAPTER TWO 12–23
    Improving Vocabulary Skills

CHAPTER THREE 24–37
    Enhancing Reading Comprehension

CHAPTER FOUR 38–43
    Developing Spelling Skills

CHAPTER FIVE 44–49
    Exploring Language Mechanics

CHAPTER SIX 50–59
    Improving Language Usage

CHAPTER SEVEN 60–67
    Utilizing Mathematical Computations

CHAPTER EIGHT 68–77
    Learning Math Concepts and Applications

CHAPTER NINE 78–83
    Interpreting Maps, Charts, and Diagrams

CHAPTER TEN 84–90
    Applying Library Skills

ANSWER KEY 91–95

INTRODUCTION

Because we are becoming a nation of "test takers," it is increasingly important that children are trained to improve skills that will allow them to be successful in taking standardized tests. National standards are being developed for all ages and for all academic areas. The best classes, schools, and futures will belong to those students who develop and improve the best test-taking techniques.

The purpose of this book, therefore, is to assist teachers and parents in preparing students to improve achievement scores. While achievement scores do not always indicate students' true knowledge or ability, parents and teachers working together on the test-taking strategies and skills in this book will find that the students' achievement scores will improve. Since there are many different types of tests administered in schools, it is important that students understand some strategies and skills so that their true knowledge is reflected on all achievement tests.

Furthermore, an improvement in achievement scores will reflect a positive reinforcement in self-confidence, creating an improved performance in all areas of academic work. This book provides some strategies and exercises for improving skills in grades 3 and 4: listening, learning to follow directions, reading comprehension, spelling, language arts, and mathematical concepts and computations.

CHAPTER ONE:
TEACHING TEST-TAKING AND STUDY SKILLS

In order to improve your test scores, remember the following:

1. Listen to your teacher as he or she explains the directions for the test.

2. Carefully read all of the directions.

    - Practice reading these key words:

directions	bubble
correct	space
STOP	fill in
GO ON	none

3. Ask any questions you may have about the test before you begin.

4. Mark your answers correctly.

    - Fill in the answer space completely.　　○ ● ○　(Yes)

    - Mark only one answer.　　● ● ○　(No)

    - Make your mark dark and solid.　　⌀ ○ ○　(No)

TEACHING TEST-TAKING AND STUDY SKILLS

Learning how to listen is a valuable study skill. By listening, we can learn to recognize sounds, words, phrases, and sentences. We need to know how to listen when following directions. Developing good listening skills and learning how to follow directions will help students do better in school and benefit them throughout their lives.

LISTENING TO DIRECTIONS:

ACTIVITY: (Teacher or Parent): Read aloud the following paragraph. Then instruct your class or child to draw a picture of a farm according to the list of directions you read. Have each child draw his or her picture on a piece of blank paper.

>Some American children live on farms. A farm is located in the country. On a farm are many different animals, a house, a barn, and a pond or a lake. On a blank sheet of paper, draw a picture of a farm by following these directions.

1. Write the title **THE FARM** at the top of your blank sheet of paper.
2. Draw a farmhouse in the middle of the paper.
3. Draw a barn in the upper right corner of the paper.
4. Add a pasture in the upper left corner of the paper.
5. Draw a road leading to the front of the house.
6. Now add a lake or a pond to the lower right corner of the paper.
7. Color the barn red.
8. Color the pasture green.
9. Color the house yellow. Color the roof of the house brown.
10. Draw some chickens, a horse, and two cows.
11. Color the animals any color you wish.
12. Draw a tractor near the barn and color it green.
13. Draw and color some flowers in the front of the house.

STOP

TEACHING TEST-TAKING AND STUDY SKILLS

IMPROVING LISTENING SKILLS AND LEARNING TO FOLLOW DIRECTIONS

ACTIVITY: As your teacher or parent reads the following paragraph, listen carefully to the directions and respond to the instructions in the space provided below.

A home aquarium can be interesting and educational. The aquarium includes a glass tank, a filtering system, a heater, a light, and a thermometer. The filter is used to keep the water clean, and the heater keeps the water at a certain desired temperature. A person can enjoy a variety of colorful, tropical fish for many years if the aquarium is properly maintained.

1. Write the word AQUARIUM at the top of the space.
2. Draw a large aquarium within the space.
3. Add a filter, heater, and thermometer.
4. Draw different kinds of fish.
5. Color the fish.
6. Add rocks or gravel at the bottom of the aquarium.
7. Draw and color different kinds of plants.

TEACHING TEST-TAKING AND STUDY SKILLS

IMPROVING LISTENING SKILLS AND LEARNING TO FOLLOW DIRECTIONS

ACTIVITY: As your teacher or parent reads the following paragraph, listen carefully to the directions and respond to the instructions in the space provided below.

MY BEDROOM

Pretend the space above is your bedroom. This drawing includes a window, bed, and nightstand. Complete the bedroom scene by responding to the following instructions.

1. Add a bookcase with books, games, and a computer.
2. Draw a lamp somewhere in the room.
3. Add your favorite picture to the wall.
4. Draw a pair of your favorite shoes. Color them brown.
5. Draw a chair and color it.
6. Add a rug or color the carpet.
7. Color the curtains and the bedspread.

TEACHING TEST-TAKING AND STUDY SKILLS

LEARNING TO FOLLOW DIRECTIONS AND IMPROVING RESEARCH SKILLS

ACTIVITY: As your teacher or parent reads the following paragraphs, listen carefully and then respond to the instructions. You may have to do some research to fill in some of the blanks.

A VISIT TO BRAZIL

Brazil is located on the continent of South America. It is the fifth largest country in the world and makes up nearly half of the total area of South America.

Carnival is one of the most exciting festivals in Brazil. During the festival, Brazilians express their national pride and identity through masquerades, parades, dances, and theme parties.

The Amazon River, which is the second longest river in the world, is in Brazil. It is 4,000 miles long, and its basin covers 2,700,000 square miles.

1. Carnival is an exciting celebration in Brazil. Write the name of a North American celebration. _____
2. The Amazon River is the second longest river in the world. Write the name of the longest river in North America. _____
3. The Brazilians are known for their colorful costumes. Color the costumes in the picture below.
4. Brazil is the largest country in South America. What is the largest state in the United States? _____
5. In the lower right corner of the picture, write the name that might belong to this dancer.

CHAPTER TWO:
IMPROVING VOCABULARY SKILLS

The last chapter introduced various test-taking tips and study skills. This chapter examines strategies that will help students to better understand and improve their use of words, including word sound, word structure, context clues, and the use of the dictionary.

PRACTICING SYNONYMS

ACTIVITY: For each question below, you are to decide which one of the four answers has the same meaning as the word in bold (heavy type) above it. Fill in the bubble next to the word with the same meaning.

TIP *Think carefully about the meaning of the word in bold print before you select an answer.*

1. The **empty** house
   - ○ very large
   - ○ vacant
   - ○ noisy
   - ○ quiet

2. **Repaired** the wall
   - ○ painted
   - ○ knocked down
   - ○ mended
   - ○ walked

3. The **unselfish** man
   - ○ strong
   - ○ neighborly
   - ○ generous
   - ○ stingy

4. A **vicious** animal
   - ○ well-behaved
   - ○ sleepy
   - ○ tamed
   - ○ mean

IMPROVING VOCABULARY SKILLS

PRACTICING CONTEXT CLUES

ACTIVITY: Complete each sentence on the left with a word from the list on the right. Use each word only once, and cross out a word after you use it.

1. China is a large _____.
2. My teacher is a kind _____.
3. Susan is my best _____.
4. The _____ was so green.
5. I _____ I can answer all the questions.
6. Please drink all of your _____.
7. Could you _____ every word she said?
8. Have you fed your _____ today?
9. Please read that _____ again.
10. Atlanta is a very big _____.
11. We had hamburgers for _____ today.
12. My family rode the _____ to Montana.
13. Thirteen is my favorite _____.
14. Did you _____ with the teacher's comment?
15. My favorite color is _____.
16. The colors do not _____.
17. Our fourth grade class visited the _____.
18. I _____ all of the word problems.
19. _____ is the coldest season.
20. December is my favorite _____.

A. agree
B. believe
C. city
D. country
E. dog
F. friend
G. grass
H. hear
I. know
J. lunch
K. match
L. milk
M. month
N. number
O. person
P. red
Q. train
R. winter
S. word
T. zoo

IMPROVING VOCABULARY SKILLS

PRACTICING WORD RECOGNITION SKILLS

ACTIVITY: Choose the correct homonym to complete each sentence.

TIP *Homonyms* are words that sound alike but are spelled differently.

1. I tasted a _____ of the pecan pie. **piece   peace**
2. Chris was _____ two dollars for returning the book late. **find   fined**
3. Susan was delayed at school for one _____ . **hour   our**
4. Nancy came _____ to visit my cousin. **buy   by**
5. My mother had to sift the _____ in order to make the cakes. **flour   flower**
6. Rob _____ the ball to the third base player. **through   threw**
7. Can your dog _____ the shrill sound? **hear   here**
8. Mrs. Cook asked us to _____ a paragraph about our favorite animal. **right   write**
9. Do you know which _____ we should take at the intersection? **road   rode**
10. Deborah sang a _____ song at the school's talent contest. **great   grate**
11. Mrs. McCoy presented three of her students with _____ ribbons. **blew   blue**
12. On our family vacation last summer, we saw a _____ in the park. **dear   deer**
13. Can you _____ me at the mall by seven o'clock? **meet   meat**
14. Has the postman delivered the _____ ? **male   mail**
15. My _____ baked several cakes for our class bake sale. **aunt   ant**

IMPROVING VOCABULARY SKILLS

MATCHING SYNONYMS

ACTIVITY: Match each word in Group B to its synonym in Group A by writing the letter on the blank line provided. **Synonyms** are words that have almost the same meaning.

A

___ 1. start
___ 2. lady
___ 3. shut
___ 4. silent
___ 5. noise
___ 6. rug
___ 7. thought
___ 8. questioned
___ 9. walk
___ 10. study
___ 11. wealthy
___ 12. incorrect
___ 13. finish
___ 14. shy
___ 15. scared
___ 16. dinner
___ 17. sad
___ 18. foolish
___ 19. town
___ 20. stay
___ 21. complete
___ 22. talk

B

a. rich
b. quiet
c. wrong
d. remain
e. sound
f. stroll
g. afraid
h. begin
i. silly
j. asked
k. supper
l. close
m. city
n. end
o. carpet
p. speak
q. finish
r. woman
s. learn
t. bashful
u. idea
v. unhappy

IMPROVING VOCABULARY SKILLS

USING ANTONYMS

ACTIVITY: After each word below there are listed three words. Choose the antonym of each word from the list and write it in the blank space provided.

TIP *Words that have opposite meanings are called **antonyms**.*

1. quit — begin, stop, end _____
2. rainy — wet, damp, sunny _____
3. happy — sad, cheerful, glad _____
4. summer — fall, spring, winter _____
5. young — old, childlike, new _____
6. early — wait, out, late _____
7. safe — trouble, shaky, dangerous _____
8. rude — nice, polite, sweet _____
9. awake — rested, sleeping, alert _____
10. hard — simple, easy, plain _____
11. light — heavy, large, strong _____
12. teach — read, learn, study _____
13. black — gray, light, white _____
14. few — little, much, many _____
15. begin — start, continue, quit _____
16. more — add, some, less _____
17. dull — pointed, sharp, rough _____
18. break — fix, tear, hurt _____
19. outside — under, up, inside _____
20. freeze — melt, chill, ice _____

IMPROVING VOCABULARY SKILLS

PRACTICING SYNONYMS, ANTONYMS, AND HOMONYMS

ACTIVITY A. Write a synonym for each word below.

TIP *Synonyms are words with similar meanings.*

1. below _____
2. fast _____
3. reason _____
4. look _____
5. silent _____
6. complete _____
7. correct _____
8. race _____
9. woman _____
10. keep _____

ACTIVITY B. Write an **antonym** for each word below.

TIP *Antonyms are words with opposite meanings.*

1. warm _____
2. happy _____
3. smile _____
4. give _____
5. good _____
6. forget _____
7. empty _____
8. teach _____
9. pull _____
10. cold _____

ACTIVITY C. Write a **homonym** for each word below.

TIP *Homonyms are words that sound alike.*

1. two _____
2. right _____
3. rode _____
4. son _____
5. weak _____
6. deer _____
7. night _____
8. pear _____
9. flour _____
10. would _____

IMPROVING VOCABULARY SKILLS

UNDERSTANDING WORDS AND THEIR MEANINGS

ACTIVITY: For each question, decide which one of the four answers has almost the same meaning as the word in heavy type above it.

1. He jumped **over** the wall.
    a. near
    b. below
    c. above
    d. beneath

2. My uncle is a famous **journalist.**
    a. storyteller
    b. news reporter
    c. politician
    d. quiz show host

3. The man gave a **firm** handshake.
    a. strong
    b. unusual
    c. friendly
    d. weak

4. We will have a **brief** recess.
    a. quiet
    b. short
    c. wild
    d. active

5. Mother **soaked** her feet.
    a. warmed
    b. rubbed
    c. kept in water
    d. rested

6. Tom **punctured** the ball.
    a. tossed
    b. hit very hard
    c. put air into
    d. put a hole in

7. Can we **reduce** traffic?
    a. count
    b. watch
    c. lessen
    d. speed up

8. My bedroom is **spacious.**
    a. very large
    b. attractive
    c. adjoining
    d. opposite

I'm ready for a brief recess!

GO ON

IMPROVING VOCABULARY SKILLS

9. The **entire** team celebrated.
   - (a) winning
   - (b) opposing
   - (c) whole
   - (d) football

10. She was **thoroughly** prepared.
    - (a) almost
    - (b) sometimes
    - (c) completely
    - (d) never

11. Why did she **slit** the paper?
    - (a) open
    - (b) mark
    - (c) cut
    - (d) tape

12. Her family is very **wealthy**.
    - (a) happy
    - (b) rich
    - (c) dirty
    - (d) close

13. The **assistant** arrived in time.
    - (a) janitor
    - (b) helper
    - (c) teacher
    - (d) waiter

14. He made **strict** rules.
    - (a) firm
    - (b) confusing
    - (c) surprising
    - (d) silly

15. Joan wore **vivid** colors.
    - (a) nice
    - (b) bright
    - (c) white
    - (d) dark

16. We have a **faithful** dog.
    - (a) loyal
    - (b) lovely
    - (c) shy
    - (d) missing

17. Her voice was **hoarse**.
    - (a) loud
    - (b) shrill
    - (c) soft
    - (d) rough

18. Mrs. Smith is so **precise**.
    - (a) unusual
    - (b) accurate
    - (c) brief
    - (d) pretty

IMPROVING VOCABULARY SKILLS

UNDERSTANDING WORDS AND THEIR MEANINGS

ACTIVITY: Write the word that does **not** belong with the other words in the group. The first one has been done for you.

1. Sue Roberta Isabelle Tom Jennifer   _Tom_
2. carrot beans apple radish corn   _____
3. saxophone clarinet opera harp tuba   _____
4. pansy daisy rose suit gardenia   _____
5. December Thursday April May June   _____
6. arm hand elbow window leg   _____
7. hammer screwdriver wheel wrench   _____
8. Billy Anthony Brenda Harry Mike   _____
9. teachers principals nurses horse   _____
10. October Monday Tuesday Thursday   _____

PRACTICING CONTRACTIONS

ACTIVITY: Complete each sentence by adding a contraction. The first one has been done for you.

TIP *A contraction is formed by putting two words together and leaving out one or more letters. An apostrophe (') is used in place of the missing letters.*

1. The doors to the school _aren't_ locked today.
2. The man in the dark gray suit _____ hear us.
3. _____ been looking for you for at least an hour.
4. The yellow brick house _____ for sale.
5. My brother Tommy _____ called yet.
6. _____ read this story in Mrs. Moody's class.
7. Why _____ you written your grandmother?

IMPROVING VOCABULARY SKILLS

MATCHING CONTRACTIONS

ACTIVITY: Match the contractions on the left with the words they represent on the right.

_m_ 1. weren't   a. I am

___ 2. I've   b. she will

___ 3. that's   c. it is

___ 4. she'll   d. did not

___ 5. haven't   e. he is

___ 6. didn't   f. who is

___ 7. what's   g. I have

___ 8. you're   h. we have

___ 9. I'm   i. can not

___ 10. hasn't   j. have not

___ 11. who's   k. would not

___ 12. wouldn't   l. you are

___ 13. it's   m. were not

___ 14. can't   n. they are

___ 15. wasn't   o. do not

___ 16. he's   p. what is

___ 17. they're   q. are not

___ 18. aren't   r. that is

___ 19. we've   s. was not

___ 20. don't   t. has not

IMPROVING VOCABULARY SKILLS

PRACTICING SYNONYMS

ACTIVITY: Find the one word that means the same as the underlined word. Fill in the answer space next to your choice.

1. a <u>valid</u> answer
   - ○ correct
   - ○ incorrect
   - ○ ridiculous
   - ○ happy

2. <u>tremble</u> at the sight
   - ○ shake
   - ○ shout
   - ○ feel
   - ○ laugh

3. to <u>declare</u> a winner
   - ○ choose
   - ○ change
   - ○ state
   - ○ find

4. test with <u>countless</u> problems
   - ○ difficult
   - ○ satisfactory
   - ○ very many
   - ○ worthless

5. a <u>wise</u> woman
   - ○ kind
   - ○ talented
   - ○ smart
   - ○ patient

6. the <u>scheme</u> of things
   - ○ need
   - ○ plan
   - ○ success
   - ○ routine

7. a very <u>talented</u> ballerina
   - ○ modest
   - ○ unusual
   - ○ skillful
   - ○ excellent

8. a <u>foolish</u> man
   - ○ sensible
   - ○ silly
   - ○ brave
   - ○ reasonable

GO ON

IMPROVING VOCABULARY SKILLS

9. predicting the weather
   - ○ forecasting
   - ○ talking
   - ○ watching
   - ○ seeing

10. has maximum potential
    - ○ minimum
    - ○ greatest
    - ○ lacking
    - ○ exciting

11. to exchange the video
    - ○ return
    - ○ purchase
    - ○ swap
    - ○ look

12. the accurate report
    - ○ cloudy
    - ○ correct
    - ○ moderate
    - ○ great

13. a piece of valuable jewelry
    - ○ expensive
    - ○ useless
    - ○ beautiful
    - ○ cheap

14. a furious teacher
    - ○ nice
    - ○ happy
    - ○ angry
    - ○ unusual

15. the frail little girl
    - ○ strong
    - ○ weak
    - ○ silly
    - ○ brave

16. the daily routine
    - ○ everyday
    - ○ unusual
    - ○ occasional
    - ○ difficult

17. her speech was brief
    - ○ long
    - ○ boring
    - ○ exciting
    - ○ short

18. a careless driver
    - ○ good
    - ○ reckless
    - ○ cautious
    - ○ happy

CHAPTER THREE:

ENHANCING READING COMPREHENSION

Learning to understand what we read is one of the most important skills that we ever learn. Because we read so much information throughout our lives, it is important to understand or comprehend what is being read. This chapter presents some activities designed to improve students' skills in reading comprehension.

READING TO UNDERSTAND

ACTIVITY: Read the following story. Then complete each sentence below by choosing the correct answer based on the information presented in the story.

ANOTHER PLANET

My furry friends Lee-la and Ramonee live on the planet Vemoora with their parents. Their father drives a gravity truck, and their mother works at a space-age delicatessen. Vemoora is a beautiful, very warm planet located in the next solar system. On Vemoora there are few trees, except for the tall cactus-looking ones with hairy thorns. Last year my family and I visited Vemoora during our summer vacation. We rented a space-age vehicle and hired a driver to take us on the 36-hour trip from Earth to Vemoora.

1. Vemoora is _____.
   - ○ my friend's name
   - ○ the airport's name
   - ○ the planet's name
   - ○ my friend's dad's name

2. It takes _____ hours to get to Vemoora.
   - ○ 36
   - ○ 24
   - ○ 12
   - ○ 35

3. Lee-la and Ramonee are _____.
   - ○ furry cactus trees
   - ○ my friends' parents
   - ○ two planets
   - ○ my furry friends

ENHANCING READING COMPREHENSION

READING TO UNDERSTAND

ACTIVITY: Read the following story. Then answer each question by filling in the circle of the best answer. If you have any problems, ask your teacher or parents for help.

FRIENDS

Jorge and Adam are good friends. Both of them are of medium height, but they don't look alike. Jorge is from Spain, and he has dark eyes and dark hair. Adam is from Oklahoma, and he has light hair and fair skin.

Adam and Jorge are the same age. They have some of the same interests in music, sports, and friends. Some of their friends include Jason, Monica, and Buddy. While Jorge enjoys playing soccer, Adam enjoys playing in the school band.

Both boys are good students. They always do their homework and both speak up in class discussions. Furthermore, they plan to attend college after graduating from high school.

1. Which boy is from Spain?
   ○ Adam
   ○ Jason
   ○ Jorge
   ○ Buddy

2. Which boy plays in the band?
   ○ Buddy
   ○ Jason
   ○ Jorge
   ○ Adam

3. Which boy is from Oklahoma?
   ○ Adam
   ○ Buddy
   ○ Jorge
   ○ Jason

4. What are Jorge's plans after high school?
   ○ go back to Spain
   ○ travel with Adam
   ○ attend college
   ○ get a job

5. Who is the boys' friend?
   ○ Leanne
   ○ Melissa
   ○ Monica
   ○ Jamie

6. Who plays soccer?
   ○ Jason
   ○ Monica
   ○ Adam
   ○ Jorge

ENHANCING READING COMPREHENSION

READING TO UNDERSTAND

ACTIVITY: Read the story below. Then answer the following questions by filling in the circle of the best answer. Don't forget to ask if you need help.

AT THE BEACH

I go to the beach in Florida every summer with my parents. We always have a lot of fun in the water and on the beach. The sun is usually hot, the water is warm, and I see many new things.

Last summer at the beach, I saw a marlin that someone had caught out in the ocean. It was about six feet long with fins that were about two feet long. On the end of its nose was a long pointed spear. In the bright sunlight, the marlin glistened and radiated a deep purple color, not black. It was so beautiful.

Every summer at the beach I always see different kinds of fish. The summer before last I saw a shark, but I wasn't afraid. It wasn't very big. I wonder what I will see next summer at the beach.

1. Which state does the person in the story visit each summer?
   - ○ Alabama
   - ○ Georgia
   - ○ California
   - ○ Florida

2. What did the person see at the beach last summer?
   - ○ friends
   - ○ sea turtles
   - ○ marlin
   - ○ shark

3. How long was the marlin?
   - ○ two feet long
   - ○ six feet long
   - ○ not too big
   - ○ eight feet long

4. What color was the marlin in the sun?
   - ○ purple
   - ○ black
   - ○ blue
   - ○ maroon

5. What did the person see on the beach the summer before last?
   - ○ shark
   - ○ marlin
   - ○ sea turtles
   - ○ red snapper

6. Where was the marlin caught?
   - ○ in the river
   - ○ near the shore
   - ○ in the ocean
   - ○ in an aquarium

ENHANCING READING COMPREHENSION

READING TO UNDERSTAND

ACTIVITY: Read the following story and then answer the following questions by filling in the circle of the best answer.

DON'T PICK THE WILDFLOWERS

Wildflowers belong in Nature's living room. They are the decorations for the earth that make our lives more beautiful. Some of the wildflowers include daisies, goldenrod, violets, honeysuckle, and mountain laurel. These flowers are for everyone to enjoy, so if you pick them you are depriving someone else of their beauty.

Wildflowers grow in the woods, along the highways and under bridges, and in our state and national parks; however, many people plant them in their yards around their houses. So the next time you see and admire a beautiful wildflower, don't pick it; let the next person enjoy it too.

1. Which word in the story goes along with daisies, violets, and honeysuckle?
   - O wild roses
   - O dandelions
   - O mountain laurel
   - O wild azalea

2. The word decorations refers to which word in the story?
   - O Christmas ornaments
   - O pumpkins and fruit
   - O popcorn chains and silver tinsel
   - O wildflowers

3. Which word in the story sounds like lime?
   - O chime
   - O time
   - O mime
   - O dime

4. To which word does the word They refer?
   - O wildflowers
   - O park rangers
   - O Smokey Bear and his friends
   - O Nature's living room

ENHANCING READING COMPREHENSION
READING TO UNDERSTAND

ACTIVITY: Read the following story and then answer the questions on the next page by filling in the circle of the best answer. If you need help, ask your teacher or parents.

COLUMBUS DISCOVERS AMERICA

As a young boy, Christopher Columbus lived in Italy. He had always had an interest in ships and sailing, so at the age of nineteen he went to sea.

He thought perhaps he could find a short cut to the Indies by sailing west, but no one was willing to take the risk of giving him money to find out. Finally, however, Columbus convinced King Ferdinand and Queen Isabella of Spain that he could find the short cut. At last they agreed, and he set sail in three ships, the *Santa María*, the *Pinta*, and the *Niña*.

After a long and restless voyage, Columbus landed in North America in October, 1492. The beautiful land that he named San Salvador is located in Latin America between Mexico and South America.

ENHANCING READING COMPREHENSION

QUESTIONS ON "COLUMBUS DISCOVERS AMERICA"

1. Who gave Columbus the ships?
   - ○ Queen Elizabeth
   - ○ King George
   - ○ Queen Isabella
   - ○ Prince Charles

2. In what country did Columbus grow up?
   - ○ Spain
   - ○ England
   - ○ San Salvador
   - ○ Italy

3. What was the name of one of the ships?
   - ○ *Pintos*
   - ○ *Santa María*
   - ○ *Niños*
   - ○ *Santa Marie*

4. Where did Columbus land in North America?
   - ○ San Salvador
   - ○ Spain
   - ○ Italy
   - ○ Florida

5. To where was Columbus looking for a shorter route?
   - ○ San Salvador
   - ○ Alaska
   - ○ Indies
   - ○ Spain

6. Which country gave Columbus the three ships?
   - ○ Italy
   - ○ America
   - ○ San Salvador
   - ○ Spain

ENHANCING READING COMPREHENSION

READING TO UNDERSTAND

ACTIVITY: Read the following poem and then answer the following questions by filling in the circle of the best answer.

THE STAGE IS SET

by Cheryl Harrison

The stage is set.
Frozen and shimmering with each twinkle of light,
She appears from the shadows
Bringing the audience to their feet with delight.
The music begins.
With great beauty and style,
She glides across the ice.
Graceful as a swan,
She moves eloquently about.
As the volume and pace increase.
She prepares for the turn of her life.
Dreams once so far away,
Now lay just beyond.
Taking flight, she soars as an eagle,
Ending like a feather, floating gently back to the frozen pond.

1. What is the person doing in the poem?
   ○ swimming   ○ flying
   ○ skating   ○ acting

2. Where is the action in the poem taking place?
   ○ on a stage   ○ in the air
   ○ at the symphony   ○ on the ice

3. Who does the word **she** refer to in the poem?
   ○ swan   ○ skater
   ○ eagle   ○ pond

ENHANCING READING COMPREHENSION

READING TO UNDERSTAND

ACTIVITY: Read the following story and then answer the questions on the following page by filling in the circle of the best answer.

THE LINE

by Jon Freeman

As I reach out my hands for the door, it opens automatically, and I feel like a fool. I stroll in nonchalantly and pick up a buggy which has a tendency to hit everything on my right.

The store is crowded and I see several people I know. I wave casually to them and continue on my way. I find the first few items on the list without any trouble, but the last two have names that make me feel illiterate. After some struggle, I find these and look for a spot in line.

I do not have many groceries, so I locate the express line. When I reach the line, a slew of people jump in front of me and another slew get behind me.

"Great," I think. "I am stuck here between all these people."

I am assailed by a strong odor. It is the smell of someone's sweat and someone else's perfume. It is a repulsive odor and I clench my nose to block it out. I break out in a cold sweat and I look around me. "What's taking so long?" my brain screams inside my head. I begin to look around as if I am being pursued by someone.

It seems like forever before I put my groceries onto the belt, and by this time, my head is spinning around and around.

I pay for the groceries and I get my change. I make a run for the door and I don't bother to stick my hands out this time. I hit the door with a hard thump, and as I fall down, I notice a sign that reads, "Pull." As a crowd gathers, I think, "Why don't things ever change?"

ENHANCING READING COMPREHENSION

QUESTIONS ON "THE LINE"

1. Where does this story take place?
   - ○ in a department store
   - ○ in a grocery store
   - ○ in a hardware store
   - ○ in a candy store

2. Why does the person fall down as he leaves the store?
   - ○ He ran into the store manager.
   - ○ He ran into a buggy in the aisle.
   - ○ He ran into the door.
   - ○ He ran into a group of people.

3. As he stands in line, what does he smell?
   - ○ cologne
   - ○ onions
   - ○ bread
   - ○ sweat

4. How does he enter the store?
   - ○ through the window
   - ○ by the elevator
   - ○ through the automatic door
   - ○ in a buggy

5. What did he bring with him into the store?
   - ○ perfume
   - ○ candy
   - ○ buggy
   - ○ list

GO ON

ENHANCING READING COMPREHENSION

DRAWING CONCLUSIONS

ACTIVITY: Read each story below and then complete the sentences from the list of words that are shown

TIP *Often you will have to draw your own conclusions when all the facts are not given.*

WORD LIST: thesaurus, sleep, conductor, teacher, musician, beautiful, fun, sadness, dictionary, grief, gray

Story 1: For the past two days, John has been coming to school with a tired look on his face. Also, he doesn't seem to be as active as he usually is. John probably needs _____ .

Story 2: Julia is writing a short story in her fourth grade English class. Her teacher told her to find another word for interesting, because Julia uses the word too much. Julia needs to look in a _____ to find another word.

Story 3: Jeremy began taking piano lessons in the first grade. He is now in the fourth grade. If he continues taking piano, and if he continues practicing, one day he may become a great _____ .

Story 4: The sky is blue. The temperature is very warm, and the wind is gently blowing. It looks as if it is going to be a _____ day.

Story 5: For months we have been planning for this day. Today, our class is attending the art museum. We are going to see paintings, drawings, sculpture, special exhibits by kids our age, and lots more. For lunch we are planning to have a big picnic in the city park where we can play games and ride the roller coaster. This day will be lots of _____ .

ENHANCING READING COMPREHENSION

READING FOR INFORMATION

ACTIVITY: Read the informative paragraphs below. Then answer the questions by filling in the circle of the best response.

A tree is a very beautiful creation in nature. It is a nest for birds, a shade for people and animals, and an ornament for the earth.

The tree is a living thing made up of roots, trunk, branches, and leaves. As the tree grows and gets older, it gets larger, just as we humans do. However, there is one part of the tree that is not alive and does not grow. This part is called the bark.

The bark of a tree protects the tree from harm, including injury and disease. The bark is the tough outer covering, sometimes appearing to be rough on some trees and smooth on others.

Even though the bark is a protective covering, we should do our best to protect our trees so that they can live a healthy life as we do.

1. What is the best title for the paragraphs above?
   ○ The Life of a Tree
   ○ The Parts of a Tree
   ○ A Lovely Tree
   ○ The Bark of a Tree

2. Which part of a tree is not a living thing?
   ○ trunk
   ○ leaves
   ○ bark
   ○ roots

3. Where is the bark found?
   ○ inside the tree
   ○ under the ground
   ○ outside the leaves
   ○ outside covering the tree

4. The bark is used for what purpose?
   ○ protect from injury and harm
   ○ protect from leaves
   ○ protect from too much sunshine
   ○ protect from air

ENHANCING READING COMPREHENSION

READING FOR DETAILS

ACTIVITY: Read the following paragraph. Then answer the questions by filling in the circle of the best answer.

HEART OF DIXIE

Alabama, a southern state, is known as the Heart of Dixie. The state's flag is white with a single red X. The most popular vacation spot in the state is the NASA (National Aeronautics and Space Administration) Space and Rocket Museum, the world's largest space museum. The museum is located in Huntsville, a city of about 240,000 people, in the northern part of the state. A major feature of the NASA facility is Space Camp, where kids have fun and learn about the space program.

1. What is one of the colors found on the Alabama flag?
   - ○ green
   - ○ white
   - ○ yellow
   - ○ blue

2. What is a popular feature of the NASA museum?
   - ○ Space and Rocket Museum
   - ○ Heart of Dixie
   - ○ Space Camp
   - ○ infrared layout of the planets

3. Where is the NASA Space and Rocket Museum located?
   - ○ in southern Alabama
   - ○ at Cape Kennedy
   - ○ in Houston, Texas
   - ○ in northern Alabama

4. In what part of the United States is Alabama located?
   - ○ southern
   - ○ northern
   - ○ eastern
   - ○ western

5. For what do the letters in NASA stand?
   - ○ North Alabama Space Administration
   - ○ National Aeronautics and Space Administration
   - ○ Northern Administration of Space Adventures
   - ○ North America Space Association

ENHANCING READING COMPREHENSION

READING FOR INFORMATION

ACTIVITY: Read the following paragraph and then answer the questions by filling in the circle of the best response.

SALVADOR DALI

Salvador Dali, a famous Spanish artist, was born in 1904 and died in 1989. His last name is pronounced as if it is spelled dah-lee. Dali said that a motivating force in his painting was fantasy. Dali was a surrealist painter; furthermore, he is considered to be one of the great surrealist painters of the twentieth century. Dali not only lived and painted in Spain, but he also studied in Paris. While in Paris, he studied with Sigmund Freud, another great figure of the twentieth century, who analyzed dreams.

1. In which country was Salvador Dali born?
   - France
   - Paris
   - Spain
   - South America

2. How does one pronounce Dali's last name?
   - dol-ly
   - dah-lee
   - da-ee
   - doll-lee

3. To what school of painting does Dali belong?
   - Cubism
   - Impressionism
   - Realism
   - Surrealism

4. Whom did Dali meet when he lived and painted in Paris?
   - Picasso
   - Freud
   - Monet
   - Van Gogh

ENHANCING READING COMPREHENSION

READING AND COMPREHENDING A LETTER

ACTIVITY: The following letter was written by someone who bought a bicycle, took it home, and then discovered that one of the rims was bent. Read the letter and then answer the questions that follow by filling in the circle of the best response.

1513 Clinton Avenue
Erlanger, KY 41018

May 27, 1995

Mr. L. T. Hinds
Mountain Bikes, Inc.
1200 Piedmont Road
Atlanta, Georgia 30345

Dear Mr. Hinds:

On May 20, I was on vacation in Atlanta with my parents. While there, I bought a mountain bike from your store because I thought it was such a great deal and I had been looking for a bike like the one I bought. However, when I arrived home and began riding the bike, I noticed that it didn't ride as it should. I took it to a bike dealer here in Erlanger, but the manager said I should contact you instead. The manager said the bike might need some major repairs.

Please tell me what I need to do. I need my bike repaired or my money back so that I can buy another one.

Sincerely,

Tommy Barnes

---

1. Where does Tommy live?
   - Atlanta
   - Erlanger
   - Miami
   - Fort Worth

2. For whom did he buy the bike?
   - for his dad
   - for his mom
   - for himself
   - for his sister

3. Why was Tommy in Atlanta?
   - working
   - hospital
   - vacation
   - school

4. What did the store manager in Erlanger advise?
   - fix the bike
   - write the company
   - take the bike home
   - trade the bike

CHAPTER FOUR:

DEVELOPING SPELLING SKILLS

The purpose of this chapter is not to teach the process of spelling but rather to refine the student's ability to proof for misspelled words. Experience has shown that the spelling section of major achievement tests is geared toward the student's choosing from a series of words either the one word that is correctly spelled or the one that is incorrectly spelled.

The exercises in this chapter have been carefully chosen to take the student step-by-step through the process of learning to proof for spelling errors with speed and accuracy. Please note that the worksheets in the final part of the chapter are based on formats the student will be exposed to on various standardized achievement tests. Feel free to use some or all of the formats as your situation requires.

ACTIVITY (Teacher or Parent): Write the following groups of words on a sheet of paper or on the chalkboard. Be sure to include the letters that precede the words.

1. What is the letter that represents the **misspelled** word in this group of words?

   A. beleive   B. fought   C. though   D. woman

2. What is the **correctly** spelled word in this group of words?

   A. brane   B. laffing   C. handel   D. safely

Repeat this type of activity, using words of your choice, until the student (class) is comfortable with these concepts.

DEVELOPING SPELLING SKILLS

RECOGNIZING MISSPELLED WORDS

ACTIVITY: Read the words in each exercise and look for a spelling mistake. In the answer rows, fill in the circle for the word with a mistake. If you do not find a mistake, mark your answer **No mistakes**.

 *Look quickly for a word that looks wrong. Sometimes all of the words are spelled correctly. Then, use **No Mistakes**.*

A.
① togithur
② double
③ children
④ No mistakes

B.
① there
② February
③ sintince
④ teeth

C.
① ghost
② choice
③ word
④ nieghbor

D.
① guess
② interest
③ friend
④ No mistakes

E.
① money
② sandwhich
③ laugh
④ enough

F.
① message
② outside
③ remoove
④ No mistakes

G.
① electric
② rolling
③ waiting
④ No mistakes

H.
① pichure
② straight
③ no one
④ let's

I.
① spread
② blackboard
③ helth
④ rebuild

J.
① improveing
② acting
③ dropped
④ No mistakes

GO ON

DEVELOPING SPELLING SKILLS

K.
1. worried
2. damage
3. bigest
4. No mistakes

L.
1. swimm
2. quickly
3. forever
4. strike

M.
1. cattle
2. certain
3. beyond
4. suppoze

N.
1. libraries
2. patiense
3. ceiling
4. No mistakes

O.
1. taking
2. receiving
3. closing
4. No mistakes

P.
1. sertain
2. careful
3. besides
4. thirteen

Q.
1. suddenly
2. collecting
3. dissapoint
4. enjoyment

R.
1. special
2. utensil
3. gentle
4. No mistakes

S.
1. misspell
2. subgect
3. dishonest
4. personally

T.
1. envelopes
2. geometry
3. exercise
4. spoonfull

U.
1. presint
2. inexpensive
3. welcome
4. rectangle

DEVELOPING SPELLING SKILLS

RECOGNIZING MISSPELLED WORDS

ACTIVITY: Read each set of words. Fill in the bubble for the word that is **misspelled**.

1. careing carrying staying
2. guide kamera gentle
3. orchard worried fryed
4. librarian terkey tomorrow
5. enjoied buying leaving
6. anxious frantic playyed
7. mammoth meazure fierce
8. pathatic prairie partner
9. breathe Tuesday seperated
10. detective effort immpressed
11. shakking nuisance pasture
12. landlord tenent pantry
13. orange height yelow
14. proffessional display blizzard

DEVELOPING SPELLING SKILLS

RECOGNIZING CORRECTLY SPELLED WORDS

ACTIVITY: Fill in the circle of the word that is spelled correctly and best completes the sentence.

1. Chip did the _____ by himself.
   - ○ exjercise
   - ○ exyercise
   - ○ exsercise
   - ○ exercise

2. Mrs. Farmer drew a _____ on the chalkboard.
   - ○ cirkle
   - ○ circle
   - ○ circal
   - ○ circkle

3. I certainly agree with your _____ .
   - ○ statemant
   - ○ staitment
   - ○ statement
   - ○ statment

4. Mom says _____ time to go.
   - ○ it's
   - ○ its
   - ○ its'
   - ○ i'ts

5. Juan was born in _____ .
   - ○ Januarry
   - ○ Jonuary
   - ○ January
   - ○ Januarie

6. Heather's cousin has opened a new _____ .
   - ○ busyness
   - ○ business
   - ○ businesst
   - ○ beesiness

7. My teacher doesn't _____ late work.
   - ○ accept
   - ○ excepte
   - ○ acept
   - ○ accepte

8. _____ tastes good.
   - ○ Lemonide
   - ○ Lemunade
   - ○ lemoniade
   - ○ Lemonade

GO ON

DEVELOPING SPELLING SKILLS

9. These science books are _____ .
   - ○ there's
   - ○ their's
   - ○ they're
   - ○ theirs

10. Shad has a new _____ of shoes
    - ○ pear
    - ○ peir
    - ○ pair
    - ○ paire

11. Everyone needs a good ____.
    - ○ fiend
    - ○ friend
    - ○ freeind
    - ○ freend

12. Jeremiah had an _____ to go to Mexico.
    - ○ oppertoonity
    - ○ oppertunity
    - ○ opportunity
    - ○ opportoonity

13. Anabelle broke her left _____ .
    - ○ shoulder
    - ○ showlder
    - ○ sholeder
    - ○ showldher

14. _____ is required to do difficult math problems.
    - ○ Patienst
    - ○ Patience
    - ○ Patiance
    - ○ Patients

15. Kaj _____ a shirt with his money.
    - ○ brougth
    - ○ buyght
    - ○ bought
    - ○ balght

16. Mohammed will _____ his parents to go.
    - ○ convence
    - ○ convinse
    - ○ convincee
    - ○ convince

17. Natasha has a character of great _____ .
    - ○ kwalitee
    - ○ qualitee
    - ○ quality
    - ○ quallity

18. If you have a _____ , perform it well.
    - ○ duty
    - ○ dooty
    - ○ duety
    - ○ dutie

CHAPTER FIVE:
EXPLORING LANGUAGE MECHANICS

It is important to learn how to communicate with one another through the use of spoken and written language. It is through proper mechanical usage that we understand and relate to each other. When we study and understand our language, expression in written form becomes easier. Therefore, we must learn and understand our language in the written form if we are to live and work together.

The purpose of this chapter is to develop and improve mechanical skills. The exercises have been chosen with an emphasis on punctuation and capitalization. By working through these exercises, students can improve their language mechanics skills as well as foster a sense of pride and confidence in their language and themselves.

PRACTICING PUNCTUATION

ACTIVITY: Read the following sentences and decide which one, if any, has an error in punctuation. Fill in the circle next to the sentence that is incorrect.

1. ○ Is everyone going to see
   ○ the movie how much
   ○ money should we bring?
   ○ No mistakes

2. ○ I cant find the book I
   ○ checked out. Maybe my
   ○ mother returned it already.
   ○ No mistakes

3. ○ Art has been around for
   ○ thousands of years. the
   ○ ancient Egyptians used art
   ○ as a way to communicate.

EXPLORING LANGUAGE MECHANICS

PRACTICING PUNCTUATION

ACTIVITY: Read the following sentences. Fill in the bubble next to the punctuation mark that is needed to make the sentence complete.

1. Jacques said, "Do you want to go to the soccer game"
   ○ .   ○ ,   ○ none   ○ ?

2. Heronda said that she would be here at 9:00.
   ○ ?   ○ none   ○ :   ○ ,

3. I am going to Yellowstone National Park next summer with my parents but my grandparents aren't going with us this year.
   ○ ,   ○ :   ○ ;   ○ none

4. Please bring to class tomorrow the following supplies pencils, paper, crayons, glue.
   ○ ;   ○ none   ○ :   ○ ,

PRACTICING PUNCTUATION

ACTIVITY: Read the following sentences. Fill in the bubble next to the line that has an error in punctuation.

1. ○ may I go with Tom to
   ○ the movie? Bill and
   ○ Ellie are going. We
   ○ always have fun together.

2. ○ Have you been to Tulsa?
   ○ My aunt lives there she has
   ○ lived there for two years with
   ○ her golden retriever Jake.

3. ○ Fabio came to visit us in
   ○ Seattle Washington last
   ○ summer. He loves soccer
   ○ very much and plays well.

4. ○ "What time is practice
   ○ tomorrow" asked Jill. "I may
   ○ be late because my history
   ○ teacher wants to see me."

EXPLORING LANGUAGE MECHANICS

PRACTICING PUNCTUATION

ACTIVITY: Read the following letter. If you find any errors in punctuation, fill in the circle next to the line in which the error is located. If there are no errors, mark **No Mistakes**.

1. ○   402 Summer Street
   ○   Huron SD 57350
   ○   May 31, 1995
   ○   (No mistakes)

2. ○ Dear Peggy
   ○   Thank you for sending me the book.
   ○ I enjoyed reading it very much.
   ○ (No mistakes)

3. ○   My class is reading the book I am
   ○ giving an oral presentation next Monday.
   ○ I hope the class enjoys the book.
   ○ (No mistakes)

4. ○   I hope to hear from you soon.
   ○   Love

   ○   Ted
   ○   (No mistakes)

PRACTICING PUNCTUATION

ACTIVITY: Read the following sentences. In each group, fill in the circle next to the sentence that has been **correctly** punctuated.

1. ○ Do you enjoy swimming in the lake in the summertime.
   ○ The plumber was here again today to fix the sink,
   ○ My speech in class yesterday was one of the best I've given.
   ○ She said, "I cant stay."

2. ○ Ashley went to London England to visit his relatives.
   ○ His grandmother lives in St. Cloud, Florida.
   ○ Did she once live in Germany.
   ○ She also lived in Valencia Spain.

EXPLORING LANGUAGE MECHANICS

PRACTICING PUNCTUATION AND CAPITALIZATION

ACTIVITY: Read the following sentences. In each group, fill in the circle next to the sentence that has been **correctly** punctuated

1. ○ Mary asked, "Where is Lapeer, Michigan."
   ○ He said it is near Detroit,
   ○ Would you like to visit sometime during the summer.
   ○ We could see the historic home on Rue Lane Drive.

2. ○ There are, apples, oranges, and pears on the kitchen table.
   ○ Dana would you help me with this problem?
   ○ Are you going to the open house, Jonah?
   ○ My friend Josh lives in New York,

3. ○ Is Norton close to Richmond in Virginia.
   ○ "I've been to Richmond?" shouted Sherry.
   ○ He said, "give me a ride to the public library, please."
   ○ "Get out of here!" joked the announcer.

PRACTICING MECHANICS

ACTIVITY: Read the following sentences. Fill in the bubble next to the line which contains an error. If there are no errors, mark **No mistakes**.

1. ○ The sun shining so warm.
   ○ Tonight I am going with her.
   ○ His birthday is January 29.
   ○ No mistakes

2. ○ Call me in the morning at 600.
   ○ I want to jog before I catch the
   ○ bus for school. Don't forget.
   ○ No mistakes

3. ○ My friends nickname is Bill,
   ○ but his real name is William.
   ○ Bill is my good friend.
   ○ No mistakes

4. ○ Kip said he would be back
   ○ in time for the rodeo, but he
   ○ hasn't returned home yet.
   ○ No mistakes

5. ○ I received a letter from Loic
   ○ in Paris. It was mailed on
   ○ Dec. 5 1994, from Paris.
   ○ No mistakes

6. ○ I bought a book on birds at
   ○ the bruno's that
   ○ recently opened at the mall.
   ○ No mistakes

EXPLORING LANGUAGE MECHANICS

USING CORRECT PUNCTUATION AND CAPITALIZATION

ACTIVITY: Read the following paragraph. As you complete the exercises, fill in the bubble next to each line which corrects the mistake found in the numbered lines of the paragraph.

The Olympics have become one of the world's major sports
1. events. The Olympics began in <u>greece in 776 b.c.</u> Many cities
2. have hosted the Olympics, such as <u>munich, seoul, and lake placid</u>.
3. In 1996, the Olympics will be held in <u>Atlanta a</u> rapidly growing city
4. found in the <u>southeastern united states</u>.

1. ○ Greece in 776 b.c.
   ○ greece in 776 B.C.
   ○ Greece in 776 B.C.
   ○ Greece in 776 BC

2. ○ munich, seoul, and Lake Placid.
   ○ Munich, seoul, and Lake Placid.
   ○ Munich, Seoul, and Lake Placid.
   ○ munich, Seoul, and Lake Placid.

3. ○ Atlanta, a
   ○ atlanta, a
   ○ atlanta a
   ○ Atlanta. A

4. ○ Southeastern United States.
   ○ southeastern United States.
   ○ southeastern, United States.
   ○ Southern united States.

USING CORRECT PUNCTUATION AND CAPITALIZATION

ACTIVITY: Read the following sentences. Fill in the bubble next to the line which shows an error in punctuation or capitalization.

1. ○ Clayton and Rico have been
   ○ friends for years now. Rico
   ○ attends Salt Lake City
   ○ elementary school.

2. ○ We are having a Scouts'
   ○ meeting on Wednesday
   ○ night. may I give you a
   ○ ride to the meeting?

3. ○ My dad and I had lunch
   ○ at McDonald's. I ordered
   ○ a big mac and a large
   ○ order of french fries.

4. ○ Disney World is located
   ○ in florida, one of my
   ○ favorite states. I hope to
   ○ visit again soon.

EXPLORING LANGUAGE MECHANICS

USING CORRECT PUNCTUATION AND CAPITALIZATION

ACTIVITY: Read the following letter. Pay attention to the punctuation and capitalization. As you complete the exercises, fill in the bubble next to each line which corrects the error found in the numbered lines in the letter. If a line from the letter is already correct, mark the circle next to the word **correct**.

---

1.   May 29 1995

2.   Dear Cynthia

3.   I am returning the costume i borrowed
4.   from you Thank you very much.

5.   Your friend

                                           Susan

---

1. ○ May 29, 1995
   ○ may 29, 1995
   ○ may 291995
   ○ correct

2. ○ dear Cynthia,
   ○ Dear Cynthia,
   ○ Dear cynthia,
   ○ correct

3. ○ costume, i
   ○ costume I
   ○ costume, I
   ○ correct

4. ○ you. Thank
   ○ you, Thank
   ○ you, thank
   ○ correct

5. ○ your Friend,
   ○ your friend,
   ○ Your friend,
   ○ correct

CHAPTER SIX:
IMPROVING LANGUAGE USAGE

We learn how to communicate better with one another by exploring and improving our language skills. Furthermore, we learn to appreciate and understand people better through the proper usage and expression of words.

The purpose of this chapter is to help students learn to express their ideas correctly and more effectively. The exercises have been carefully chosen with an emphasis on language usage and expression. By diligently working through these exercises, students will improve their language skills both in the classroom and in their everyday lives.

UNDERSTANDING LANGUAGE USAGE

ACTIVITY: Read the following sentences. Fill in the bubble next to the line which contains an error in usage. If there are no errors, then mark the bubble **No mistakes**.

1. ○ When Harry first met Sally,
   ○ they didn't like each other.
   ○ Now, they is good friends.
   ○ No mistakes

2. ○ He don't like to go outside
   ○ after dark because he heard
   ○ a strange noise the other night.
   ○ No mistakes

3. ○ Pat swam out in the lake
   ○ to the most deepest part.
   ○ Then, he swam back.
   ○ No mistakes

4. ○ Karisa is practicing her
   ○ favorite jumps for the
   ○ competition tomorrow.
   ○ No mistakes

©1996 by Incentive Publications, Inc., Nashville, TN.

EXPLORING LANGUAGE USAGE

UNDERSTANDING LANGUAGE USAGE

ACTIVITY: Read the following sentences. Fill in the bubble next to the line which does not contain any errors.

1. ○ What's for supper tonight?
   ○ Did Martha get a gift for she?
   ○ The flower don't bloom red.
   ○ Her flowers is blooming too.

2. ○ He had wrote a nice letter.
   ○ I ain't had so much fun.
   ○ The children worn their caps.
   ○ She had driven the car before.

3. ○ This is gooder than yours.
   ○ Is she taller than him?
   ○ Is he smaller than she?
   ○ Dad bought one for you and I.

4. ○ The mother birds brings insects.
   ○ Anthony are a happy little fellow.
   ○ Buying the house was lots of fun.
   ○ Jim and me may go fishing.

5. ○ I don't have no money.
   ○ He doesn't hardly know.
   ○ Ted didn't get no food.
   ○ Doesn't anybody know?

6. ○ Mrs. Bly is gonna go.
   ○ Driving the car fast.
   ○ This is more whiter.
   ○ Laughing, they jumped.

7. ○ He has taking it before.
   ○ She did it you do it too.
   ○ It got out of it's cage.
   ○ I hope to meet him.

UNDERSTANDING LANGUAGE USAGE

ACTIVITY: Read the following sentences. Fill in the bubble next to the line which contains an error in usage. If there are no errors, then mark the bubble **No mistakes**.

1. ○ Me and Michael enjoy Salvador
   ○ Dali's artwork. Michael once did
   ○ some research on Dali's life.
   ○ No mistakes

2. ○ Wes' family and us are going
   ○ to Nevada this winter to snow
   ○ ski. I can't wait.
   ○ No mistakes

IMPROVING LANGUAGE USAGE

FINDING THE SIMPLE SUBJECT

ACTIVITY: Read the following sentences and then fill in the bubble under the **correct simple subject**.

1. The tall <u>green</u> pine <u>trees</u> <u>reach</u> straight up to the <u>sky</u>.
   ○   ○   ○   ○

2. After <u>we</u> return from our <u>vacation,</u> <u>we</u> <u>are moving</u>.
   ○   ○   ○   ○

3. <u>There</u> are <u>apples</u> on the <u>kitchen</u> <u>table</u>.
   ○   ○   ○   ○

4. <u>Mercury</u> revolves around the <u>sun</u> once <u>every</u> eighty-eight <u>earth days</u>.
   ○   ○   ○   ○

FINDING THE SIMPLE VERB OR PREDICATE

ACTIVITY: Read the following sentences and then fill in the bubble(s) under the **correct simple verb** or **correct simple predicate**.

5. The <u>frisky</u> young <u>dogs</u> <u>ran</u> <u>around</u> in the yard.
   ○   ○   ○   ○

6. The kind <u>teacher</u> <u>had</u> <u>written</u> a <u>note</u> to her <u>parents</u>.
   ○   ○   ○   ○   ○

7. We <u>are</u> <u>not</u> <u>going</u> to the <u>movie</u> <u>tonight</u>.
   ○   ○   ○   ○   ○

8. <u>David</u> <u>knew</u> the path <u>along</u> the river <u>very</u> well.
   ○   ○   ○   ○

©1996 by Incentive Publications, Inc., Nashville, TN.

IMPROVING LANGUAGE USAGE

UNDERSTANDING PARAGRAPH STRUCTURE

ACTIVITY: Read the following paragraphs. Pay close attention to the sentences in each paragraph. If a sentence does not belong in the paragraph, fill in the bubble of the numbered sentence that does not belong.

1. (1) I have a pet iguana that lives out behind our house. (2) Every day I see him and take him bits of food. (3) My friend Llana has a pet kangaroo that visits his patio every evening right before sundown. (4) I have named my iguana Isley because of the funny way he moves his eyes.

   - A. Sentence 1
   - B. Sentence 2
   - C. Sentence 3
   - D. Sentence 4

2. (1) The owl is a night predator. (2) Its eyesight allows it to see and capture its food at night. (3) Often one can hear an owl hooting at night as it sits perched high in a tree waiting for potential prey. (4) My grandfather's rooster doesn't hunt food at night; he sleeps in the top of the tall oak tree behind the barn.

   - A. Sentence 1
   - B. Sentence 2
   - C. Sentence 3
   - D. Sentence 4

3. (1) Kites are flown all over the world and have been part of customs throughout history. Boys' Day is May 5 in Japan. Every family flies a carp kite for each boy in its family. (2) The carp is a fish which is a symbol of courage and success. (3) I have a kite which I won as a prize at my school's yard sale. Kites' Day is celebrated in China on the ninth day of the ninth month. The kites are in the shapes of birds, butterflies, and dragons. (4) The kites in China and Japan represent good luck and good fortune for each family's household.

   - A. Sentence 1
   - B. Sentence 2
   - C. Sentence 3
   - D. Sentence 4

IMPROVING LANGUAGE USAGE

UNDERSTANDING PARAGRAPH STRUCTURE

ACTIVITY: Read the following paragraph. If a sentence does not belong in the paragraph, fill in the bubble of the numbered sentence that does not belong.

Last July, the Coletti family had their family reunion. Aunts, uncles, and cousins came from many distant cities. (1) Uncle Leo, who traveled from Venice, Italy, came the farthest. (2) Many relatives brought their favorite dishes or recipes for everyone to share. (3) Harriet and Bill visited Europe during the month of August. Large pans of lasagna, spaghetti, and baked breads filled the tables. (4) My Uncle Harry, who owns a bakery, furnished a variety of cookies and cakes. It was great seeing all the relatives, many of whom we had not seen for years.

1. ○ A. Sentence 1 ○ C. Sentence 3
   ○ B. Sentence 2 ○ D. Sentence 4

PRACTICING SENTENCE STRUCTURE

ACTIVITY: Read the following sentences, then fill in the bubble of the sentence that states the thought most clearly.

TIP *A clearly written sentence is easy to understand. Be sure each sentence has a subject and verb and makes a complete thought.*

1. ○ A. Yesterday Sheri made dozens of chocolate chip cookies.
   ○ B. Chocolate chip cookies, Yesterday Sheri made dozens for us.
   ○ C. Yesterday dozens of chocolate chip cookies Sheri made.
   ○ D. Dozens of chocolate chip cookies, Sheri made them for us.

2. ○ A. I was going to ride my bicycle, but it was broken to school.
   ○ B. My bicycle to school couldn't be ridden because it was broke.
   ○ C. It was broken when I planned to ride my bicycle to school.
   ○ D. Because my bicycle was broken, I could not ride it to school.

3. ○ A. My mother, hamburgers and fries for lunch.
   ○ B. My mother made hamburgers and fries for lunch.
   ○ C. Made hamburgers and fries for lunch.
   ○ D. My mother made lunch she made hamburger and fries.

IMPROVING LANGUAGE USAGE

PRACTICING SENTENCE STRUCTURE

ACTIVITY: Read the following sentences. Fill in the bubble of the sentence that states the thought most clearly.

1. ○ A. To make brownies Cathy and I were trying when the electricity went off.
   ○ B. Cathy and I were trying, when the electricity went off, to make brownies.
   ○ C. When the electricity went off, to make brownies Cathy and I were trying.
   ○ D. Cathy and I were trying to make brownies when the electricity went off.

2. ○ A. In our neighborhood the children like to play with bicycles, kites, puzzles, and games.
   ○ B. To play with bicycles, kites, puzzles, and games the children like in our neighborhood.
   ○ C. With bicycles, kites, puzzles, and games the children in our neighborhood like to play.
   ○ D. The children, with bicycles, kites, puzzles, and games, in our neighborhood like to play.

UNDERSTANDING LANGUAGE USAGE AND EXPRESSION

ACTIVITY: Read the following sentences. Fill in the bubble of the word or phrase that best completes each sentence.

TIP *As you read the sentence, try each answer in place of the blank to decide which one sounds the best.*

1. The children sang ____ song.
   ○ theirs
   ○ there
   ○ their
   ○ there's

2. I ____ a party tonight.
   ○ am having
   ○ are having
   ○ having
   ○ is having

3. Please give the book to ____ .
   ○ her
   ○ she
   ○ we
   ○ our

4. John ____ his favorite shirt.
   ○ worn
   ○ wear
   ○ has wore
   ○ is wearing

IMPROVING LANGUAGE USAGE

UNDERSTANDING LANGUAGE USAGE AND EXPRESSION

ACTIVITY: Read the following sentences. Fill in the bubble of the word or phrase that best completes each sentence.

TIP *As you read the sentence, try each answer in place of the blank to decide which one sounds the best.*

1. Does San Diego get ____ than San Francisco?
   - ○ hot
   - ○ hotter
   - ○ hottest
   - ○ more hot

2. You can go to the movies, ____ you can go to the mall.
   - ○ so
   - ○ nor
   - ○ yet
   - ○ or

3. A dolphin is much ____ than a whale.
   - ○ small
   - ○ smaller
   - ○ smallest
   - ○ more small

4. Charlotte ____ her library book to her sister.
   - ○ give
   - ○ given
   - ○ has given
   - ○ has give

5. A blooming flower is ____ than an artificial one.
   - ○ pretty
   - ○ prettier
   - ○ prettiest
   - ○ most pretty

6. Rhonda is the ____ student in our class.
   - ○ tall
   - ○ taller
   - ○ tallest
   - ○ more tall

PRACTICING SENTENCE STRUCTURE

ACTIVITY: Look at the following sentences. Fill in the bubble of the sentence which is the best combination of the sentences marked with an * below.

1. * John is my best friend.
   * Jason is also my best friend.

   - ○ John is my only best friend.
   - ○ John and Jason are my best friends.
   - ○ Jason is my only best friend.
   - ○ John is my best friend at school and Jason is my best friend away from school.

IMPROVING LANGUAGE USAGE

PRACTICING SENTENCE STRUCTURE

ACTIVITY: Read the following sentences. Fill in the bubble of the sentence which is the best combination of the sentences marked with an * below.

1. * My principal's name is Mr. Finkelstein.
   * My principal has a wife and four children.
   ○ My principal, Mr. Finkelstein, has a wife and four children.
   ○ My principal's name is Mr. Finkelstein, and he has a wife and four children.
   ○ Mr. Finkelstein has a wife and four children.
   ○ My principal's name is Mr. Finkelstein who has a wife and children.

2. * I have a pet cat.
   * He is white with one black spot.
   * His name is Simon.
   ○ I have a pet cat whose name is Simon.
   ○ I have a pet cat whose name is Simon, and he is white with one black spot.
   ○ I have a pet cat, Simon, that is white with one black spot.
   ○ I have a pet cat Simon that is white.

PRACTICING PARAGRAPH STRUCTURE TOPIC SENTENCES

ACTIVITY: Read the following paragraph. Notice that the first, or topic, sentence is missing. Below the paragraph, fill in the bubble next to the sentence that you think would make the best topic sentence.

_____. He always treats me with lots of respect and understanding. Until he quit smoking his tobacco pipe, he would let me blow out his match after he lighted his pipe. Also, he always seems so glad to see me when we visit each other. I am very lucky to have a grandfather like mine.

1. ○ My grandfather has been sick lately.
   ○ My grandfather has a little vegetable garden every year.
   ○ My grandfather is the greatest man in the world.
   ○ My grandfather and grandmother have always been good to me.

IMPROVING LANGUAGE USAGE

PRACTICING PARAGRAPH STRUCTURE/TOPIC SENTENCES

ACTIVITY: Read the following paragraph. Notice that the first, or topic, sentence is missing. Below the paragraph, fill in the bubble next to the sentence you think would make the best topic sentence.

_____. My school has the best teachers in the world. My school also has a principal, Mrs. Willis, who makes us laugh and want to come to school. At my school we can play soccer, baseball, and volleyball, and we have a nature trail with a classroom in the woods. I don't plan to be absent from school at all this year, because school is great.

- ○ My school would be a great place except our lunches are bad.
- ○ My school is fun except for our mean principal Mrs. Willis.
- ○ My school is fun, but I also enjoy staying at home watching videos.
- ○ I am very proud to attend my school.

PRACTICING PARAGRAPH STRUCTURE/SUPPORTING SENTENCES

ACTIVITY: Read the following paragraph. A supporting sentence is missing. Below the paragraph, fill in the bubble next to the sentence you think keeps the paragraph flowing in an organized manner.

Martin Luther King, Jr., was a great civil rights leader during the late 1950s and 1960s in America. He traveled all over the United States speaking out and marching against racial discrimination. _____. In 1968, he was assassinated in Memphis, Tennessee. Today, because of Dr. King, African-Americans have equal rights and can expect to be treated fairly all over America.

- ○ His father lived and preached in Atlanta, Georgia.
- ○ He was married to Coretta King and they have four children.
- ○ Sometimes he was not treated kindly and fairly, and once he was put in jail for several days in Birmingham, Alabama.
- ○ I have much respect for Dr. Martin Luther King, Jr.

**MARTIN LUTHER KING DAY
is observed on the third Monday in January.**

IMPROVING LANGUAGE USAGE

UNDERSTANDING LANGUAGE USAGE AND EXPRESSION

ACTIVITY: Read the following sentences. Fill in the bubble next to the line which contains an error in usage. If there are no errors, then mark the bubble **No mistakes**.

1. ○ He don't ever come to class
   ○ with his homework. I could
   ○ never do that to myself.
   ○ No mistakes

2. ○ Grandfather is very strong.
   ○ He has broke the handle in
   ○ his garden rake again.
   ○ No mistakes

3. ○ When Jim came bouncing
   ○ into the room, the teacher
   ○ and I was discussing it.
   ○ No mistakes

4. ○ Are you ready? It is almost
   ○ time for you and me to give
   ○ our oral presentations.
   ○ No mistakes

5. ○ There is apples and oranges
   ○ on the kitchen table. Bring me
   ○ an apple, if you don't mind.
   ○ No mistakes

6. ○ Dad, can I ride the roller coaster
   ○ one more time? Jonathan has
   ○ rode three times already.
   ○ No mistakes

7. ○ The dog it was my pet
   ○ that won the competition.
   ○ We won twenty dollars.
   ○ No mistakes

8. ○ I would of gone with you,
   ○ but I had my chores to do
   ○ first. No one else can.
   ○ No mistakes

9. ○ Jennifer knowed she was
   ○ wrong, but she kept on
   ○ arguing with Ann anyway.
   ○ No mistakes

10. ○ No, I can't paint the pen.
    ○ Larry he knows how to
    ○ paint. Ask him.
    ○ No mistakes

11. ○ Have you spoken to your
    ○ pen pal lately? I speak to
    ○ mine yesterday.
    ○ No mistakes.

CHAPTER SEVEN:
UTILIZING MATHEMATICAL COMPUTATIONS

Recognizing and understanding the relationships that exist among numbers are important skills to have in our rapidly changing technological world. These skills are not difficult to learn, but everyone must know them, especially when writing and speaking, using money, and telling time.

The exercises presented in this chapter were developed to help students improve their abilities in such areas as addition, subtraction, multiplication, and division. Some students may have trouble with these concepts, so provide plenty of assistance if they are having a difficult time. However, once students master these skills, they will feel better about themselves in the classroom and be confident when approaching these concepts in a test-taking situation.

ADDITION, SUBTRACTION, MULTIPLICATION, AND DIVISION

ACTIVITY: Look at the following problems. Pay attention to the signs that tell you what to do. Fill in the bubble of the correct answer.

1. 306
   + 6
   ○ 252
   ○ 312
   ○ 321
   ○ 302

2. 306
   − 8
   ○ 298
   ○ 314
   ○ 312
   ○ 296

3. 243
   − 11
   ○ 231
   ○ 230
   ○ 232
   ○ 254

UTILIZING MATHEMATICAL COMPUTATIONS

4. 25   ○ 27
   +2   ○ 50
         ○ 23
         ○ 52

5. 42   ○ 252
   +6   ○ 48
         ○ 36
         ○ 242

6. 250 ○ 650
   +3   ○ 850
         ○ 750
         ○ 253

7. 31   ○ 89
    30   ○ 61
   +29   ○ 90
         ○ 91

8.   64 ○ 225
    122 ○ 185
   +38   ○ 224
         ○ 220

9. 120 ○ 723
    260 ○ 722
   +342 ○ 724
         ○ 720

10. 164 ÷ 4 =   ○ 41
                ○ 40
                ○ 42
                ○ 44

11. 125 ÷ 5 =   ○ 21
                ○ 20
                ○ 25
                ○ 24

12. 48 + 8 =   ○ 58
               ○ 56
               ○ 54
               ○ 59

13. 16 + 80 =   ○ 96
                ○ 95
                ○ 94
                ○ 97

14. ¾ − ¼ =   ○ 4/4
              ○ ¼
              ○ 2/4
              ○ 5/4

15. 6/8 − 2/8 =   ○ 8/8
                  ○ 4/8
                  ○ 5/8
                  ○ 7/8

STOP

UTILIZING MATHEMATICAL COMPUTATIONS

ADDITION, SUBTRACTION, MULTIPLICATION, AND DIVISION

ACTIVITY: Look at the following problems. Pay attention to the signs that tell you what to do. Fill in the bubble of the correct answer. If the answer is not given, mark **N** for **Not Given.**

1. 10 + 90 =
   - ○ 9
   - ○ 11
   - ○ 8
   - ○ N

2. 72 − 53
   - ○ 19
   - ○ 125
   - ○ 18
   - ○ 21

3. 83 − 26
   - ○ 57
   - ○ 56
   - ○ 109
   - ○ N

4. 31 × 9
   - ○ 278
   - ○ 279
   - ○ 40
   - ○ 277

5. 49 − 39
   - ○ 88
   - ○ 11
   - ○ 10
   - ○ 9

6. 76 − 58
   - ○ 134
   - ○ 18
   - ○ 16
   - ○ 17

7. 6 + 91 =
   - ○ 96
   - ○ 85
   - ○ 98
   - ○ 97

8. 400 × 7
   - ○ 2807
   - ○ 2800
   - ○ 2811
   - ○ 2828

9. 510 × 4
   - ○ 2040
   - ○ 2004
   - ○ 514
   - ○ 2440

10. 261 × 6
    - ○ 1565
    - ○ 1564
    - ○ 267
    - ○ 1566

11. 903 × 2
    - ○ 1806
    - ○ 905
    - ○ 1860
    - ○ 901

12. 34 × 3
    - ○ 102
    - ○ 37
    - ○ 31
    - ○ 103

UTILIZING MATHEMATICAL COMPUTATIONS

ADDITION, SUBTRACTION, MULTIPLICATION, AND DIVISION

ACTIVITY: Look at the following problems. Pay close attention to the signs that tell you what to do. Fill in the bubble of the correct answer. If the answer is not given, mark **N** for **Not Given**.

1. 3 x 86 =
   - ○ 248
   - ○ 158
   - ○ 328
   - ○ 258

2. 101 x 2 =
   - ○ 202
   - ○ 101
   - ○ 103
   - ○ 104

3. 100 ÷ 5
   - ○ 25
   - ○ 20
   - ○ 30
   - ○ N

4. 500 ÷ 10 =
   - ○ 20
   - ○ 25
   - ○ 50
   - ○ 40

5. 900 ÷ 30 =
   - ○ 30
   - ○ 90
   - ○ 50
   - ○ N

6. 3 x 612 =
   - ○ 1,939
   - ○ 1,836
   - ○ 1,756
   - ○ 1,693

7. 327
   + 327
   - ○ 648
   - ○ 654
   - ○ 944
   - ○ N

8. 571
   + 471
   - ○ 942
   - ○ 972
   - ○ 1,042
   - ○ 952

9. 1,517
   − 608
   - ○ 909
   - ○ 919
   - ○ 809
   - ○ N

10. 130 ÷ 5 =
    - ○ 25
    - ○ 16
    - ○ 26
    - ○ N

11. 411 x 7 =
    - ○ 2,877
    - ○ 2,777
    - ○ 2,407
    - ○ 2,111

12. 648
    −159
    - ○ 499
    - ○ 409
    - ○ 479
    - ○ 489

STOP

UTILIZING MATHEMATICAL COMPUTATIONS

ADDITION, SUBTRACTION, MULTIPLICATION, AND DIVISION

ACTIVITY: Look at the following problems. Pay close attention to the signs that tell you what to do. Fill in the bubble of the correct answer. If the answer is not given, mark **N** for **Not Given**.

1. 1012
   + 2012
   - ○ 2024
   - ○ 3024
   - ○ 3022
   - ○ 2033

2. 5600
   × 2
   - ○ 11,200
   - ○ 10,200
   - ○ 10,120
   - ○ N

3. 1246
   + 1052
   - ○ 2398
   - ○ 2298
   - ○ 2388
   - ○ 2188

4. 78 ÷ 6 =
   - ○ 18
   - ○ 15
   - ○ 13
   - ○ N

5. 96 ÷ 8 =
   - ○ 13
   - ○ 12
   - ○ 15
   - ○ 14

6. 108 ÷ 9 =
   - ○ 11
   - ○ 13
   - ○ 12
   - ○ N

7. 512 − 12 =
   - ○ 400
   - ○ 500
   - ○ 510
   - ○ N

8. 0.6 − 0.4 =
   - ○ 0.4
   - ○ 0.8
   - ○ 0.3
   - ○ N

9. 71 − 5 =
   - ○ 76
   - ○ 56
   - ○ 66
   - ○ 75

10. 5/8 + 3/8 =
    - ○ 6/8
    - ○ 2/8
    - ○ 1
    - ○ 8

11. 12 + 29 =
    - ○ 41
    - ○ 50
    - ○ 17
    - ○ N

12. 501 + 491 =
    - ○ 990
    - ○ 992
    - ○ 792
    - ○ 590

©1996 by Incentive Publications, Inc., Nashville, TN.

UTILIZING MATHEMATICAL COMPUTATIONS

ADDITION, SUBTRACTION, MULTIPLICATION, AND DIVISION

ACTIVITY: Look at the following problems. Pay close attention to the signs that tell you what to do. Fill in the bubble of the correct answer. If the answer is not given, mark **N** for **Not Given**.

1. 2 x 28 x 1 =
   - ○ 24
   - ○ 56
   - ○ 31
   - ○ 48

2. 144 ÷ 12 =
   - ○ 24
   - ○ 12
   - ○ 48
   - ○ 16

3. ½ + ½ + ½ =
   - ○ 1½
   - ○ 1¼
   - ○ 2¾
   - ○ N

4.
   ```
     50
     31
     24
   + 16
   ```
   - ○ 121
   - ○ 111
   - ○ 101
   - ○ 131

5. 420 – 102 =
   - ○ 218
   - ○ 228
   - ○ 220
   - ○ 318

6. 777 x 2 =
   - ○ 1544
   - ○ 1554
   - ○ 1455
   - ○ 1557

7. 96 ÷ 6 =
   - ○ 16
   - ○ 56
   - ○ 31
   - ○ 26

8. $\frac{9}{12} - \frac{8}{12} =$
   - ○ $\frac{4}{12}$
   - ○ $\frac{1}{12}$
   - ○ $\frac{5}{12}$
   - ○ $\frac{6}{12}$

9.
   ```
     1000
     3009
   + 2101
   ```
   - ○ 5110
   - ○ 7010
   - ○ 6110
   - ○ 6010

10. 128 ÷ 8 =
    - ○ 24
    - ○ 16
    - ○ 32
    - ○ 42

11. 2320 x 5 =
    - ○ 11,600
    - ○ 56,000
    - ○ 31,000
    - ○ 48,600

12. 9 x 12 =
    - ○ 108
    - ○ 118
    - ○ 119
    - ○ N

13. 84 ÷ 3 =
    - ○ 24
    - ○ 26
    - ○ 31
    - ○ 28

14. ½ x ¼ =
    - ○ ⅙
    - ○ ¼
    - ○ ⅛
    - ○ N

15. 24 + 16 + 8 =
    - ○ 58
    - ○ 56
    - ○ 40
    - ○ 48

16. 3000 ÷ 5 =
    - ○ 500
    - ○ 600
    - ○ 400
    - ○ 650

UTILIZING MATHEMATICAL COMPUTATIONS

MULTIPLICATION AND DIVISION

ACTIVITY: This activity is to see how well you can compute. Work all the problems on a separate sheet of paper; then, decide which of the four answers for each problem is correct. If the correct answer is not given, NG (NOT GIVEN) is the correct answer. Circle the letter of the answer that is correct.

1. 25 x 9 =
   a. 222   c. 225
   b. 125   d. 325

2. 96 x 2 =
   a. 192   c. 292
   b. 98   d. NG

3. 83 x 4 =
   a. 87   c. 332
   b. 232   d. 79

4. 56 x 2 =
   a. 54   c. 58
   b. 212   d. 112

5. 23 x 8 =
   a. 183   c. 182
   b. 181   d. NG

6. 44 x 3 =
   a. 131   c. 232
   b. 132   d. NG

7. 58 x 3 =
   a. 174   c. 172
   b. 234   d. NG

8. 55 x 5 =
   a. 270   c. 575
   b. 60   d. 275

9. 70 x 6 =
   a. 420   c. 720
   b. 76   d. NG

10. 51 x 4 =
    a. 55   c. 204
    b. 224   d. 222

11. 62 x 6 =
    a. 472   c. 374
    b. 68   d. 372

12. 61 x 17 =
    a. 1037 c. 1036
    b. 78   d. NG

13. 22 x 33 =
    a. 716   c. 755
    b. 736   d. 726

14. 12 x 36 =
    a. 422   c. 432
    b. 372   d. 156

15. 59 x 13 =
    a. 767   c. 556
    b. 72   d. 768

16. 40 x 23 =
    a. 1009 c. 63
    b. 980   d. 920

17. 45 ÷ 3 =
    a. 12   c. 15
    b. 16   d. NG

18. 400 ÷ 5 =
    a. 80   c. 20
    b. 35   d. NG

19. 335 ÷ 5 =
    a. 65   c. 35
    b. 72   d. 67

20. 654 ÷ 6 =
    a. 96   c. 108
    b. 109   d. NG

21. 615 ÷ 3 =
    a. 205   c. 310
    b. 215   d. NG

STOP

UTILIZING MATHEMATICAL COMPUTATIONS

ADDITION, SUBTRACTION, MULTIPLICATION, AND DIVISION

ACTIVITY: This activity is to see how well you can compute. Work all the problems on a separate sheet of paper; then, decide which of the four answers for each problem is correct. If the correct answer is not given, NG (NOT GIVEN) is the correct answer. Circle the letter of the answer that is correct.

1. 275
    × 6
    a. 1560
    b. 1650
    c. 1555
    d. NG

2. 6220
    − 5219
    a. 910
    b. 751
    c. 1001
    d. NG

3. 475 ÷ 5 =
    a. 85
    b. 75
    c. 95
    d. NG

4. $ 3.23
    2.96
    + 3.75
    a. $9.92
    b. $9.96
    c. $8.94
    d. NG

5. ⅝ + ⅝ =
    a. 1½
    b. 1¼
    c. 1¾
    d. NG

6. 342 × 3 =
    a. 1024
    b. 926
    c. 1026
    d. NG

7. 890
    − 620
    a. 250
    b. 270
    c. 150
    d. NG

8. $2.23
    + 3.29
    a. $5.51
    b. $4.52
    c. $5.52
    d. NG

9. 1830 ÷ 30 =
    a. 60
    b. 65
    c. 61
    d. NG

10. 99 × 3 =
    a. 295
    b. 297
    c. 193
    d. NG

11. 1010
    + 2123
    a. 3123
    b. 4133
    c. 3133
    d. NG

12. 4/6 − 1/6 =
    a. ½
    b. ⅔
    c. ⅚
    d. NG

13. 2105 ÷ 5 =
    a. 421
    b. 420
    c. 40
    d. NG

14. $0.22
    0.78
    + 0.31
    a. $2.31
    b. $1.39
    c. $1.31
    d. $1.32

15. 555 ÷ 8 =
    a. 69 R2
    b. 69 R1
    c. 67 R3
    d. 69 R3

CHAPTER EIGHT:

LEARNING MATH CONCEPTS AND APPLICATIONS

Achievement tests place special emphasis on a student's competence in the areas of time, money, and problem solving. In recognition of this fact, Chapter 8 introduces the student to these skills in a typical test-taking situation.

The information in this chapter is presented in a variety of formats so that the student will become more comfortable with the test-taking process. Therefore, the activities in this chapter have been designed to provide the individual student with the tools necessary to be more successful on future achievement tests. Working successfully through these exercises will improve the student's sense of pride and confidence in all areas of study.

APPLYING MATH CONCEPTS

ACTIVITY: Read each of the following problems, and then fill in the circle of the correct answer.

1. Which of the following numbers is less than 6?
   ○ 6   ○ 7   ○ 8   ○ 5

2. What is the word name for 3,251?
   ○ three thousand two hundred fifty
   ○ three thousand two hundred fifty-two
   ○ three thousand two hundred fifty-one
   ○ thirty-two thousand two hundred fifty-one

3. Which shape is a triangle?

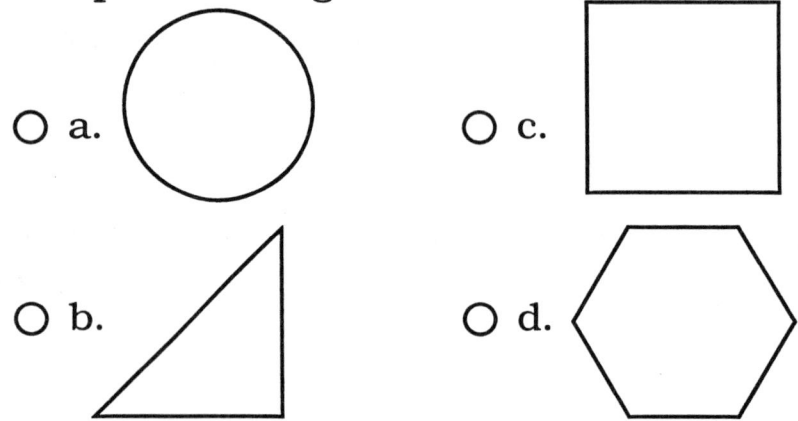

○ a.   ○ c.
○ b.   ○ d.

GO ON →

LEARNING MATH CONCEPTS AND APPLICATIONS

4. What should replace the blank in the following problem?

    5 __ 6 = 30

    ○ x ○ +
    ○ ÷ ○ −

5. The length of your pencil is probably closest to which measurement below?
    ○ 9 feet   ○ 16 inches
    ○ 8 yards   ○ 9 inches

6. What is the numeral for one thousand two hundred forty-one?
    ○ 12411   ○ 1241
    ○ 141   ○ 1242

7. What is the number that is closest in value to 38?
    ○ 40   ○ 34
    ○ 35   ○ 41

8. What is the best estimate for 32 plus 26?
    ○ 50   ○ 70
    ○ 60   ○ 20

9. What is the number needed to fill the blank in the subtraction problem?

    ```
      721
    − ___
      505
    ```
    ○ 206
    ○ 226
    ○ 116
    ○ 216

10. Which number is a factor of 54?
    ○ 17   ○ 26
    ○ 8   ○ 9

    Hello! I'm 7 tens, and 2 ones, also known as 6 tens and 12 ones. 72

11. Leanne has 6 collections of old pen sets. Each pen set has 3 pens. What is the total number of pens in all the collections?
    ○ 9   ○ 3
    ○ 18   ○ 12

GO ON

LEARNING MATH CONCEPTS AND APPLICATIONS

12. The teacher divided 36 by 3. Then he added 12 to the answer. Choose the correct formula below that shows this problem.
    - ○ 36 ÷ 3 + 12 = ?
    - ○ 36 ÷ 3 = 12
    - ○ 36 ÷ 3 x 12 = ?
    - ○ 36 ÷ 3 – 12 =

13. Jason bought some paper for $2.49. He gave the clerk $5.00. What was his change?
    - ○ $2.50
    - ○ $2.51
    - ○ $3.51
    - ○ $1.51

14. Look at the following number sequence. What number is missing?   36, ___, 42, 45, 48
    - ○ 38
    - ○ 37
    - ○ 40
    - ○ 39

15. How many of the following numbers are less than 176? 175, 177, 179, 169, 174
    - ○ 2
    - ○ 3
    - ○ 4
    - ○ 1

16. What is the following shape called?
    - ○ cone
    - ○ triangle
    - ○ cube
    - ○ rectangle

17. Complete the following equation:
    2 x 6 = 24 ÷ ___ ?
    - ○ 2
    - ○ 3
    - ○ 12
    - ○ 6

18. If you divide each number below by 4, which number will have a remainder?
    - ○ 36
    - ○ 24
    - ○ 92
    - ○ 27

19. In the following subtraction problem, what number is missing?

    ```
        ?
      - 606
      -----
       206
    ```
    - ○ 806
    - ○ 412
    - ○ 812
    - ○ 612

LEARNING MATH CONCEPTS AND APPLICATIONS

APPLYING MATH CONCEPTS

ACTIVITY: Read each of the following problems, and then fill in the circle of the correct answer.

1. Which of the following numbers is 8 less than 19?
   - ○ 11
   - ○ 12
   - ○ 27
   - ○ 10

2. What part of this figure is unshaded?

   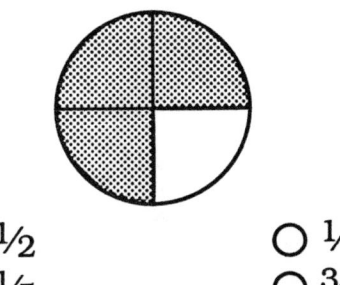

   - ○ ½
   - ○ ¼
   - ○ ⅕
   - ○ ¾

3. If 8 x N = 24, what is N?
   - ○ 16
   - ○ 32
   - ○ 2
   - ○ 3

4. Round off the answer of the following problem to the nearest ten.

   54 + 34 = ___?
   - ○ 88
   - ○ 80
   - ○ 90
   - ○ 100

5. What is another way to write 65?
   - ○ 6 x 10 + 4
   - ○ 100 ÷ 2 + 4
   - ○ 30 x 2 + 5
   - ○ 120 − 60 − 5

6. Counting by threes, which number sequence is correct?
   - ○ 150, 153, 156, 159
   - ○ 150, 152, 155, 158
   - ○ 152, 155, 157, 160
   - ○ 152, 155, 158, 160

7. Which of the following shapes is a circle?
   - ○ a.
   - ○ b.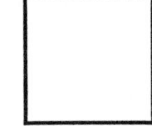
   - ○ c.
   - ○ d.

8. How many pounds are needed to balance the scale?

   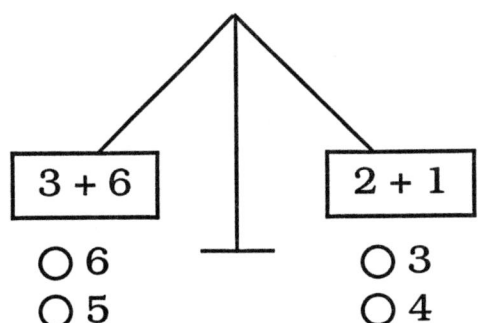

   - ○ 6
   - ○ 3
   - ○ 5
   - ○ 4

LEARNING MATH CONCEPTS AND APPLICATIONS

READING A CHART

ACTIVITY: Read the following chart closely and then fill in the circle of the best answer to each question. Study the problems closely, and don't be too hasty when filling in your answers.

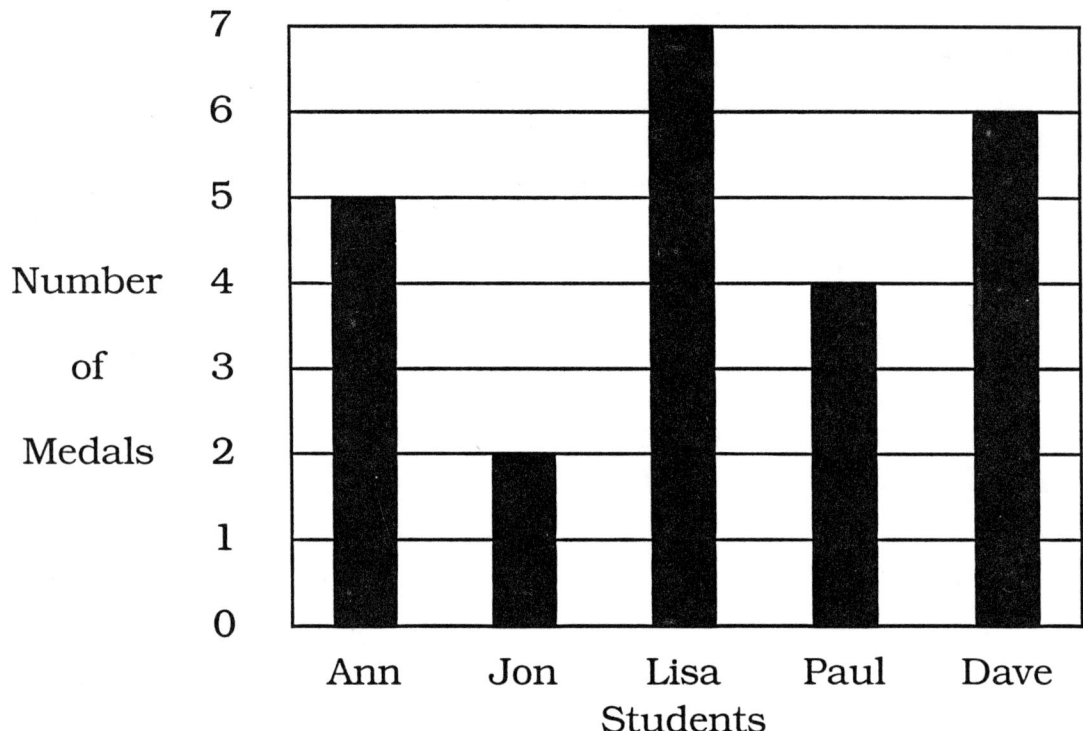

1. Which student won more than 6 medals?
   ○ Dave   ○ Ann
   ○ Lisa   ○ Paul

2. How many more medals does Jon need to have as many medals as Lisa?
   ○ 4   ○ 5
   ○ 3   ○ 2

3. What is the total number of medals won by the girls?
   ○ 18   ○ 16
   ○ 12   ○ 22

LEARNING MATH CONCEPTS AND APPLICATIONS

PRACTICING WORD PROBLEMS

ACTIVITY: Read each of the following problems closely, and then fill in the circle of the best answer. If you need help, ask your teacher or parent.

1. Marcela made tacos for her friends. She made 3 batches with 6 tacos in each batch. How many tacos did she make in all?
   - ○ 9
   - ○ 6
   - ○ 18
   - ○ 15

2. Lennie spent 3 weeks at summer camp. He left on June 1. When did he return?
   - ○ June 15
   - ○ July 1
   - ○ June 22
   - ○ June 20

3. Which of the following has the greatest value?
   - ○ 5 dimes + 3 pennies
   - ○ 2 quarters + 4 pennies
   - ○ $.52
   - ○ 1 quarter + 3 dimes

4. In $(5 + 10) \div 3 = 15 \div N$, what is N?
   - ○ 5
   - ○ 3
   - ○ 15
   - ○ 10

5. Loic bought 2 pairs of jeans for $30 each and one shirt for $20. How much did he spend in all?
   - ○ $80
   - ○ $50
   - ○ $70
   - ○ $85

6. Miss Rubino paid $1.80 for some special pencils. Each pencil cost $ .30. How many pencils did she buy?
   - ○ 5
   - ○ 6
   - ○ 7
   - ○ 4

7. On his vacation, Helmut collected 29 shells on Monday, 25 on Tuesday, and 23 on Thursday. How many shells did he collect on Tuesday and Thursday?
   - ○ 77
   - ○ 52
   - ○ 48
   - ○ 54

8. Soo bought 3 stamps for $ .32 each at the post office. She gave the lady a $1 bill. How much change did she get?
   - ○ $.01
   - ○ $.02
   - ○ $.03
   - ○ $.04

LEARNING MATH CONCEPTS AND APPLICATIONS

PRACTICING WORD PROBLEMS

ACTIVITY: Read each of the following problems carefully and then fill in the circle of the correct answer. If you need help, ask your teacher.

1. In one hour from the time shown on the clock, what time will it be?

   ○ 5:00   ○ 6:00
   ○ 3:00   ○ 4:30

2. What time does the following clock show?

   ○ 2:15   ○ 3:15
   ○ 3:10   ○ 3:00

3. Which of the following clocks shows 20 minutes after 2?

   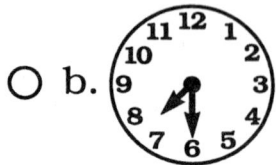   

4. George weighed 70 pounds at Christmas. By the following Thanksgiving, he had gained 23 pounds. How much did he weigh at Thanksgiving?
   ○ 73   ○ 93
   ○ 90   ○ 92

5. Raoul's dad bought 3 steaks for $2.58 each. He gave the attendant a $10 bill. How much change did he get?
   ○ $2.26   ○ $2.24
   ○ $2.25   ○ $2.27

6. Josh makes 254 doughnuts everyday at his job. If he works 5 days a week, how many doughnuts does he bake in one week?
   ○ 1070   ○ 1275
   ○ 1170   ○ 1270

7. Samantha has 14 pencils in a bag. There are 7 red, 2 white, 3 blue, and 2 purple. If she, without looking, chooses 1 pencil from the bag, which color would she most likely choose?
   ○ red   ○ blue
   ○ white   ○ purple

LEARNING MATH CONCEPTS AND APPLICATIONS

PRACTICING WORD PROBLEMS

ACTIVITY: Read each of the following problems closely, and then fill in the circle of the correct answer. Don't hesitate to ask for help.

1. The closest estimate of 321 minus 216 is what?

    ○ 500   ○ 100
    ○ 200   ○ 1000

2. The closest estimate of 424 times 3 is what?

    ○ 12,000   ○ 1200
    ○ 13,000   ○ 1500

3. The closest estimate of 1244 divided by 300 is what?

    ○ 30   ○ 4
    ○ 3   ○ 44

4. The closest estimate of 24.64 minus 21.60 is what?

    ○ 4   ○ .04
    ○ 3   ○ 46.24

5. The closest estimate of $76.24 added to $86.24 is what?

    ○ $100   ○ $2,000
    ○ $300   ○ $200

6. Mr. Juarez gave Carlos 14 homework problems. Carlos did 10 right after school. How many more did he have to do?

    ○ 6   ○ 3
    ○ 5   ○ answer not given

7. There are 20 students in Anabel's class. There are 10 times this number of students in the whole school. How many students are in the school?

    ○ 30   ○ 10
    ○ 200   ○ 2,000

8. Jake, a golden retriever, eats 50 pounds of food a month. If the food costs about $.20 a pound and if 4 weeks equals 1 month, how much will the food cost for 1 week?

    ○ $2.50   ○ $22.50
    ○ $10.00   ○ $ .225

STOP

LEARNING MATH CONCEPTS AND APPLICATIONS

READING A CHART

ACTIVITY: Read the following graph carefully. Then respond to each question below by filling in the circle of the best answer. If you have any difficulty, ask your teacher or parents for help.

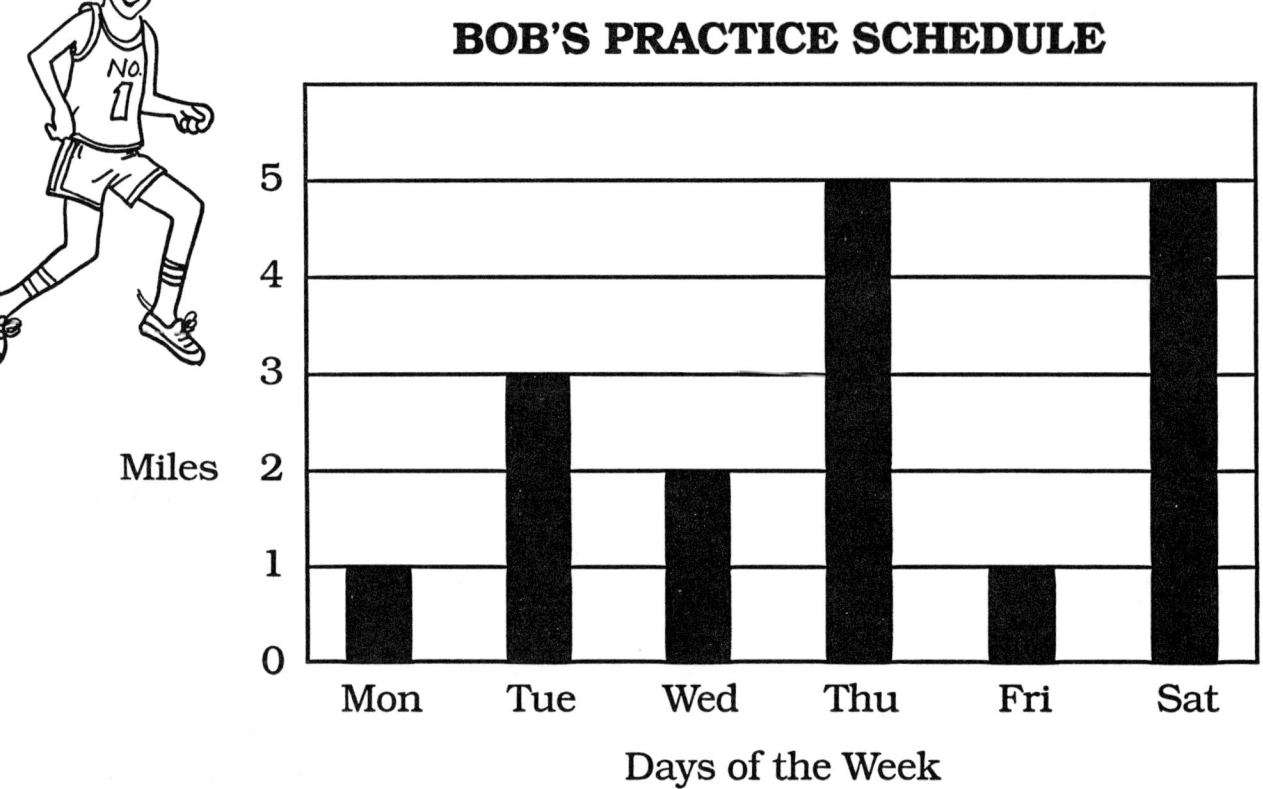

1. If Bob runs only Monday, Wednesday, and Friday, how many miles does he run?
    - ○ 4
    - ○ 9
    - ○ 7
    - ○ 14

2. If Bob runs every day, how many miles does he run?
    - ○ 14
    - ○ 17
    - ○ 9
    - ○ 18

3. If Bob runs only Tuesday, Thursday, and Saturday, how many miles does he run?
    - ○ 14
    - ○ 17
    - ○ 13
    - ○ 9

STOP

LEARNING MATH CONCEPTS AND APPLICATIONS

PRACTICING WORD PROBLEMS

ACTIVITY: Read each of the following problems carefully, and then fill in the circle of the correct answer. Ask your teacher or parents if you need help.

1. If Brian is in a line of 9 people, and he is last in line, what is his place in the line?
   - ○ 9th
   - ○ 8th
   - ○ 10th
   - ○ 11th

2. What part of the following circle is shaded?

   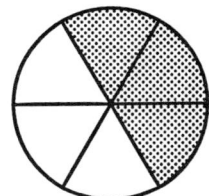

   - ○ 3/6
   - ○ 7/16
   - ○ 5/8
   - ○ 1/4

3. Which number goes in the blank to make the number sentence true?
   (5 + ____) + (2 x 4) = 4 x 4
   - ○ 2
   - ○ 5
   - ○ 3
   - ○ 6

4. Juan bought a pound of bananas at the farmers' market. He gave 3/4 of the pound to his mother. How much does he have left?
   - ○ 1/8
   - ○ 1/4
   - ○ 1/2
   - ○ 2/4

5. Caleigh thinks of a number which has a 5 in the ones place and a 7 in the tens place. Also, the number is between 300 and 400. What is the number?
   - ○ 357
   - ○ 375
   - ○ 475
   - ○ 257

6. If Alessandra slices a pie into 5 pieces and gives Lois one piece, what part of the pie did she give to Lois?
   - ○ 2/5
   - ○ 6/5
   - ○ 1/5
   - ○ 1/3

7. Lea made a party drink using 6 cups of orange juice, 2 cups of grape juice, and 2 cups of apple juice. If 1 pint equals 2 cups, then how many pints of drink did she make?
   - ○ 5
   - ○ 10
   - ○ 4
   - ○ 8

8. Bea has 267 pennies. What is another way to write this amount?
   - ○ $.267
   - ○ $26.70
   - ○ $2.67
   - ○ $.0267

CHAPTER NINE:
INTERPRETING MAPS, CHARTS, AND DIAGRAMS

Learning to read maps, charts, and diagrams is an important problem-solving skill to acquire. News reports, weather reports, current events, travel, as well as many occupations, require the ability to read and to understand maps, charts, and diagrams. Early exposure to, as well as experiences with, maps, charts, and diagrams will help children develop the basic skills needed both in school and in life. The authors, therefore, encourage parents and teachers to work through the following activities to improve a child's ability to interpret these common tools.

READING A CHART

ACTIVITY: Mrs. Culpepper's third grade class went on a nature walk in Briarlake School's Nature Park. The chart below shows some of the things each student saw on the nature walk. Study the chart, then fill in the circle in front of the best answer to each question below.

\multicolumn{6}{c	}{THIRD GRADE CLASS NATURE WALK}
STUDENT	BIRDS	BIRD NESTS	BUTTERFLIES	SQUIRRELS	WILDFLOWERS
Stephanie	6	4	10	2	11
Lauren	3	4	4	0	8
Jeff	9	5	9	2	10
Natasha	3	2	5	1	7
Kevin	8	4	7	4	4
Natalie	6	3	8	1	6
Yura	8	4	3	0	7
Malika	4	2	5	1	3

1. How many butterflies did Natalie see in the nature park?
   ○ 3   ○ 6   ○ 1   ○ 8

2. Who saw the fewest wildflowers?
   ○ Kevin   ○ Jeff
   ○ Malika   ○ Natalie

3. Which student saw the most birds?
   ○ Jeff   ○ Kevin
   ○ Yura   ○ Stephanie

4. Who saw the same number of squirrels as bird nests?
   ○ Lauren   ○ Kevin
   ○ Natasha   ○ Malika

INTERPRETING MAPS, CHARTS, AND DIAGRAMS

READING A GRAPH

ACTIVITY: Before school ended, Ms. Greer's fourth grade class spent a day at the zoo. Everyone had a great time being together, enjoying a delicious picnic, and seeing all of the animals. At the zoo, Ms. Greer's class saw zebras, elephants, kangaroos, monkeys, tigers, lions, horses, deer, bears, peacocks, and ostriches.

Study the graph carefully. Then answer the questions below.

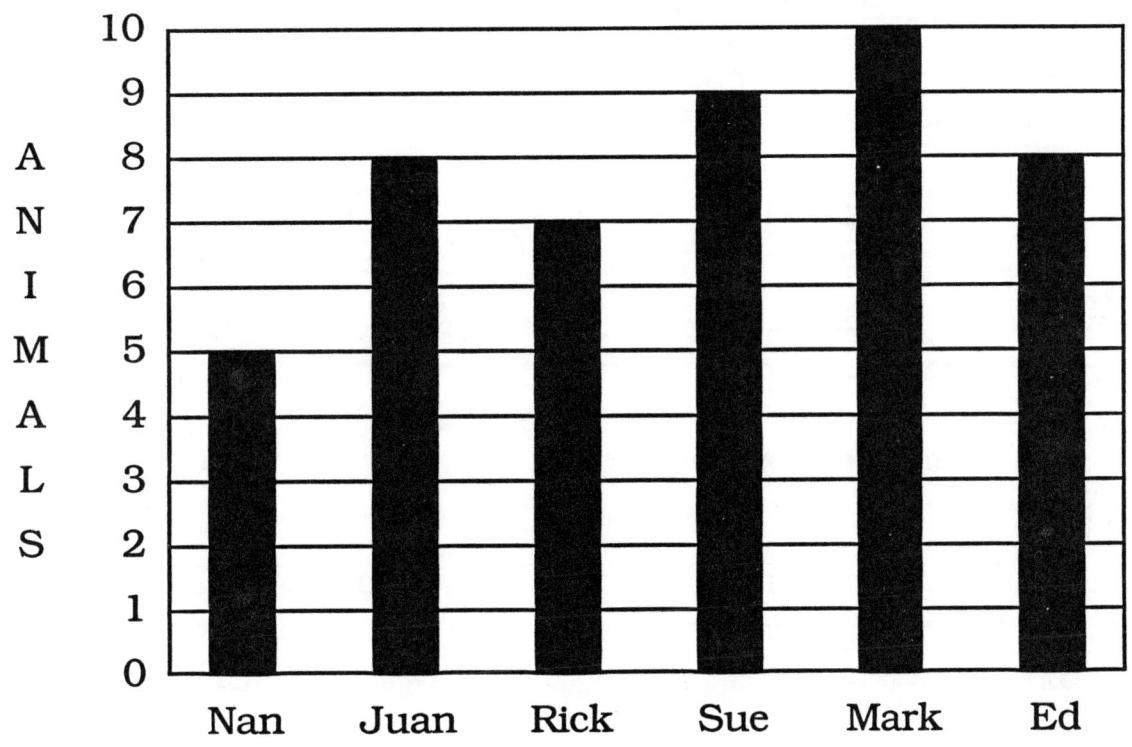

A VISIT TO THE SAN DIEGO ZOO

1. Who saw the most animals at the zoo?
   - ○ Juan
   - ○ Sue
   - ○ Mark
   - ○ Rick

2. Which student saw the least number of animals?
   - ○ Ed
   - ○ Nan
   - ○ Rick
   - ○ Sue

3. How many students saw more than 5 animals?
   - ○ 5
   - ○ 4
   - ○ 6
   - ○ 3

4. How many animals did Juan, Sue, and Mark see together?
   - ○ 22
   - ○ 29
   - ○ 24
   - ○ 27

INTERPRETING MAPS, CHARTS, AND DIAGRAMS

READING A MAP

ACTIVITY: The map above shows my neighborhood. Use this map to answer the questions below by filling in the bubble for the best answer.

1. Which of the following buildings is located on Knoll Drive?
   - a. Clayton Manor Apartments
   - b. Marcia's house
   - c. convenience store
   - d. Knight Elementary School

2. The school's playground is located on which street?
   - a. Park Avenue
   - b. Springdale Avenue
   - c. Andrews Drive
   - d. Knox Avenue

3. Tom's house is located at which intersection?
   - a. Andrews and Springdale
   - b. Park and Knoll
   - c. Andrews and Park
   - d. Andrews and Knoll

4. Bill went with his mother to the dry cleaners. If they drove west on Andrews Drive, on which street would they turn north to reach the cleaners?
   - a. Springdale Avenue
   - b. Oak Street
   - c. Park Avenue
   - d. Knoll Drive

©1996 by Incentive Publications, Inc., Nashville, TN.

INTERPRETING MAPS, CHARTS, AND DIAGRAMS

READING A MAP

ACTIVITY: Study the map of Washington, D.C., below. Four answers are given for each question. Fill in the the bubble next to the answer that you think is better than the others.

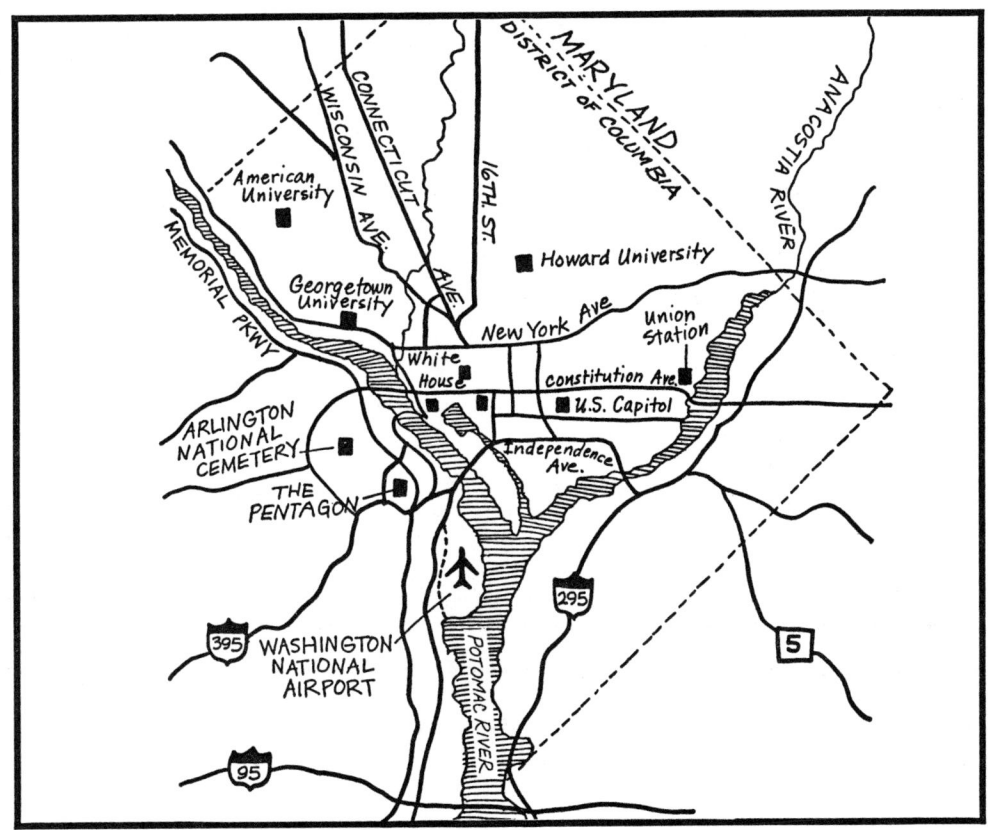

1. The Washington National Airport is located between which two interstates?
    - ○ a. Interstates 95 and 65
    - ○ b. Interstates 395 and 295
    - ○ c. Interstates 395 and 65
    - ○ d. Interstates 295 and 365

2. Which university is located on New York Avenue?
    - ○ a. Howard University
    - ○ b. American University
    - ○ c. Georgetown University
    - ○ d. University of Maryland

3. The White House is located on which street?
    - ○ a. Wisconsin Avenue
    - ○ b. Independence Avenue
    - ○ c. Connecticut Avenue
    - ○ d. Constitution Avenue

4. What famous river flows through the heart of Washington, D.C.?
    - ○ a. Anacostia River
    - ○ b. Potomac River
    - ○ c. Silver Springs River
    - ○ d. Rock Creek River

INTERPRETING MAPS, CHARTS, AND DIAGRAMS

ACTIVITY: Study the U.S. map of major cities. Then answer the questions below by filling in the circle of the best answer.

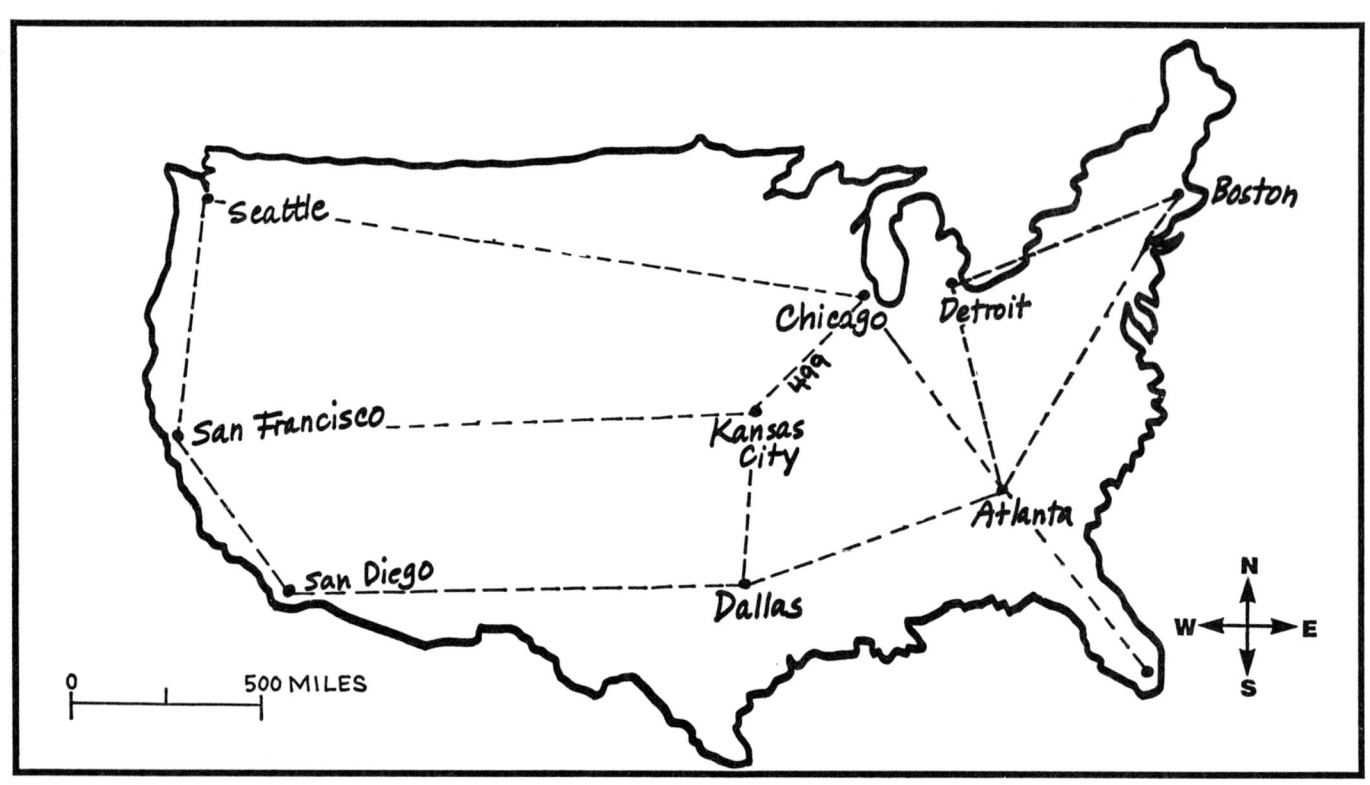

1. Estimate the distance in miles from San Francisco to Chicago if you travel through Kansas City.
   ○ a. 1,250   ○ b. 1,500   ○ c. 2000   ○ d. 2500
2. If you flew from Dallas to Boston through Atlanta, how many (estimated) miles would you travel?
   ○ a. 1,500   ○ b. 1,750   ○ c. 2,000   ○ d. 2250
3. What city on the map is almost directly north of Dallas?
   ○ a. Atlanta   ○ b. Kansas City   ○ c. San Diego   ○ d. Miami
4. On our family vacation last summer, we traveled from Boston to Detroit, then to Atlanta. How many miles did our family travel?
   ○ a. 1,250   ○ b. 1,500   ○ c. 1,750   ○ d. 2,000
5. In which direction would you go from Kansas City to San Francisco?
   ○ a. north   ○ b. south   ○ c. east   ○ d. west
6. My dad drives a truck from Seattle to Chicago for three weeks out of every month. On the fourth week, he drives from Seattle to San Francisco. What is the difference in mileage between cities for these two trips?
   ○ a. 500   ○ b. 750   ○ c. 1,000   ○ d. 1,250

STOP

INTERPRETING MAPS, CHARTS, AND DIAGRAMS

READING A MAP

ACTIVITY: Study the Oregon map below. Then answer the following questions by filling in the circle for the best answer.

1. What route would you use to travel from Prineville to Madras?
   - ○ a. 370
   - ○ b. 26
   - ○ c. 380
   - ○ d. 27

2. How many miles is it from Prineville to Madras?
   - ○ a. 27
   - ○ b. 29
   - ○ c. 56
   - ○ d. 46

3. What is the closest state park (S.P.) to Prineville?
   - ○ a. Ochoco Lake
   - ○ b. Maury Mountain
   - ○ c. Lookout Mountain
   - ○ d. Grizzly Mountain

4. What mountain chain is located due east from Bend?
   - ○ a. Mill Creek Wilderness
   - ○ c. Grizzly Mountain
   - ○ b. Lookout Mountain
   - ○ d. Maury Mountains

*Note: The numbers alongside the roads indicate miles. The circled numbers indicate routes.

5. What city is north of Bend?
   - ○ a. Prineville
   - ○ b. Redmond
   - ○ c. Post
   - ○ d. Bear Creek

6. Where is Bear Creek Butte located?
   - ○ a. west of Bend
   - ○ b. north of Redmond
   - ○ c. east of Prineville
   - ○ d. east of Bend

7. What mountain is located between Prineville and Madras?
   - ○ a. Grizzly Mountain
   - ○ b. National Maury Mountains
   - ○ c. Stephenson Mountain
   - ○ d. Diablo Mountain

STOP

©1996 by Incentive Publications, Inc., Nashville, TN.

CHAPTER TEN:
APPLYING LIBRARY SKILLS

It is important that students learn to use the library because there are so many valuable resources available that can help them in almost any kind of research. Students will encounter such resources as dictionaries, atlases, almanacs, encyclopedias, magazines, and newspapers in the library. Learning how to use these resource materials properly will make learning more fun and help save time when doing research on particular projects. Furthermore, if children feel comfortable using the library, they will become more confident as students.

USING REFERENCE SOURCES

ACTIVITY: Read the following questions and then fill in the bubble of the correct answer. If you need help, ask your teacher or parents.

1. If the teacher asked you to find the meaning of the word democracy, which book would you probably use first?

   ○ a. encyclopedia   ○ b. atlas   ○ c. dictionary   ○ d. magazine

2. If you wanted to find some general information on the life of former President John F. Kennedy, in which resource would you look?

   ○ a. atlas   ○ b. magazine   ○ c. dictionary   ○ d. encyclopedia

3. If you wanted to find a map of the little island of Macua (located near Hong Kong), in which book would you look?

   ○ a. magazine   ○ b. encyclopedia   ○ c. atlas   ○ d. dictionary

APPLYING LIBRARY SKILLS

USING THE TABLE OF CONTENTS

ACTIVITY: Using the table of contents from ***Traveling with My Students,*** answer the questions on the following page.

Volume 2

Traveling with My Students

Contents

Famous Monuments in Moscow and St. Petersburg 5

The Hermitage Museum of St. Petersburg 19

Olympic Stadium and Boycotting the Olympics 29

Walking about Red Square 40

The Red Star from Moscow to St. Petersburg 56

The Kremlin and the Government 69

Food in the Former U.S.S.R. 81

Ballet and Opera in Moscow and St. Petersburg 98

Famous Circus of Moscow 115

Peter the Great's Famous Summer Palace 127

Beautiful Architecture in St. Petersburg 145

Religion and Church in the Former U.S.S.R. 157

Getting Around in Russia 176

Museum of Atheism in Moscow 193

The People of Moscow and St. Petersburg 212

I Want to Go Back to Russia and Why 241

APPLYING LIBRARY SKILLS

1. Beginning on which page would you probably find information on the beautiful columns and architecture found in the big church in St. Petersburg?
    - ○ a. 5
    - ○ b. 157
    - ○ c. 145
    - ○ d. 212

2. If you needed information on one famous leader of Russia before it became the U.S.S.R., on what page would you begin looking?
    - ○ a. 127
    - ○ b. 176
    - ○ c. 69
    - ○ d. 40

3. If you were going to visit St. Petersburg and wanted to visit its famous art museum, which chapter would probably give you the most information?
    - ○ a. Museum of Atheism in Moscow
    - ○ b. Beautiful Architecture in St. Petersburg
    - ○ c. The Hermitage Museum of St. Petersburg
    - ○ d. Famous Monuments in Moscow and St. Petersburg

4. If you were researching information on the churches of the former U.S.S.R., under what chapter would you probably find the most material?
    - ○ a. Museum of Atheism in Moscow
    - ○ b. Religion and Church in the Former U.S.S.R.
    - ○ c. The Kremlin and the Government
    - ○ d. The People of Moscow and St. Petersburg

5. Suppose your teacher asked you to research one custom found among the people of Moscow and St. Petersburg, on which page would you begin looking?
    - ○ 40
    - ○ 69
    - ○ 241
    - ○ 212

6. If you and your friends were planning to visit Moscow and St. Petersburg and wanted to learn more about the musical arts entertainment that would be available, then you would probably begin looking in which chapter?
    - ○ a. Ballet and Opera in Moscow and St. Petersburg
    - ○ b. Getting Around in Russia
    - ○ c. The People of Moscow and St. Petersburg
    - ○ d. Walking about Red Square

APPLYING LIBRARY SKILLS

READING AN ATLAS

ACTIVITY: Look at the following map of Australia and answer the questions below.

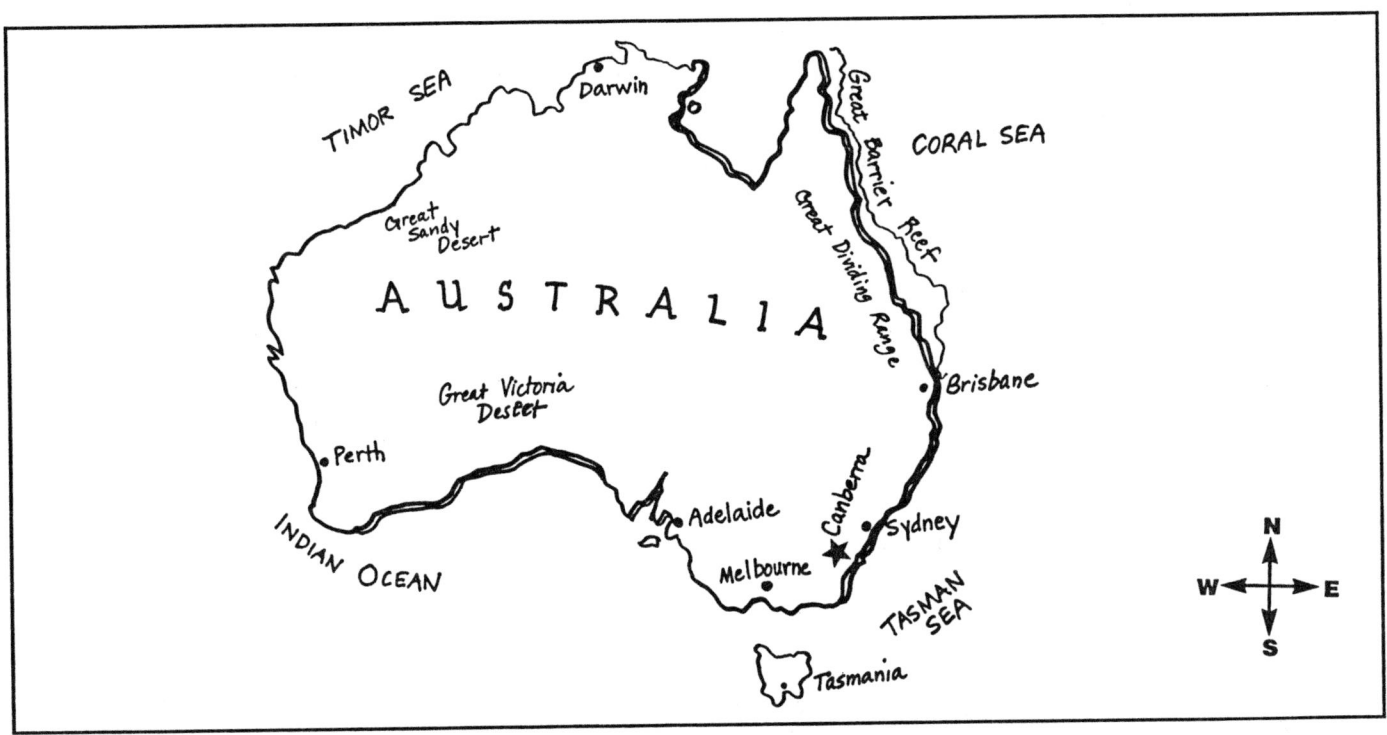

1. What is the city located on the west coast of Australia?
   - ○ Brisbane
   - ○ Adelaide
   - ○ Darwin
   - ○ Perth

2. The ☆ beside a city's name on the map means that the city is what?
   - ○ very important
   - ○ a capital
   - ○ a shipping port
   - ○ very tourist-oriented

3. What is the name of the little island located southeast of Australia?
   - ○ Tasmania
   - ○ Hobart
   - ○ New Guinea
   - ○ Indonesia

4. The Great Barrier Reef is world famous for its beautiful coral and fish. Where is the Reef located in relation to Australia?
   - ○ northwest
   - ○ north
   - ○ southeast
   - ○ northeast

5. What large body of water is located on the south-western side of Australia?
   - ○ Tasman Sea
   - ○ Coral Sea
   - ○ Timor Sea
   - ○ Indian Ocean

APPLYING LIBRARY SKILLS

READING THE DICTIONARY

ACTIVITY: Reading closely and using the following dictionary entries, answer the questions on the next page.

fun (fun) *n.* 1 playfulness, amusement, sport 2 a source of amusement *Reading is fun.* *v.* to make a joke or to play, to mock (to make fun of).

function (funk'-shən) *n.* 1 the normal action of anything 2 the duty of a person in work 3 a formal ceremony *Graduation is a function in which all seniors wish to participate.* *v.* to act in an expected manner, to work, to be used *Does this copier function as it should?*

funeral (fu'-ner-əl) *n.* 1 ceremonies related to burial or cremation of the dead 2 the procession that accompanies the body to the place of burial *As we were driving downtown, we saw a funeral drive by on its way to the cemetery.* *adj.* like, of, or suitable for burial ceremonies *The family still had to make funeral arrangements for their deceased grandfather.*

fungus (fun'-gəs) *n.* 1 a group of plants, including molds, rusts, mildews, mushrooms, etc., that have no flowers, leaves, or green color and reproduce by their spores *Look at the brown fungi growing on the dead tree.* 2 in medicine, a moldlike substance that may cause disease *pl.* fungi.

funny (fun'-i) *adj.* (-nier, -niest). 1 causing laughter, amusing, humorous 2 (colloq) out of the ordinary, strange *adv.* **funnily** *n.* **funniness**.

Furies (fyoor'-iz) *n. pl.* in Greek and Roman mythology, the three female spirits who punished people who committed unavenged crimes (crimes other than those of revenge).

furious (fyoor'-i-əs) *adj.* 1 full of intense feeling of fury, violent *The father was furious with his daughter when she arrived home late.* 2 violently overpowering *n.* **furiousness** *adv.* **furiously**.

furor (fyoor'-or) *n.* 1 rage, frenzy, fury *The badly hurt animal was in a state of furor.* 2 outburst of enthusiasm, craze.

furry (fur'-i) *adj.* (-rier, -riest) 1 of fur or made of fur 2 covered with fur or wearing fur 3 like fur, having the texture of fur *n.* **furriness**.

fuss (fus) *n.* 1 nervous state, unnecessary worry *v.* to worry, to bother *Don't fuss over things that you cannot control.*

GO ON →

APPLYING LIBRARY SKILLS

1. If someone is violent, then we say that person is what?
   - a. Furies
   - b. furry
   - c. furious
   - d. furor

2. The **u** in **furor** sounds like the **u** in which word?
   - a. urn
   - b. Furies
   - c. bun
   - d. fungus

3. Which word means "humorous"?
   - a. furry
   - b. fun
   - c. fungus
   - d. funny

4. Complete the following sentence with the correct word. **The ___ of the pencil sharpener is to sharpen the pencil.**
   - a. furor
   - b. function
   - c. fungus
   - d. fuss

5. If you saw some mildew growing on your back deck, you might conclude that it was what?
   - a. fungus
   - b. function
   - c. furry
   - d. furor

6. When the Beatles first came to America, most people who attended their concerts were crazed with excitement. Some people said that they were in a state of what?
   - a. furious
   - b. fuss
   - c. funeral
   - d. furor

7. When you get your first job, your boss will probably assign you a certain duty or _____.
   - a. furor
   - b. fungus
   - c. function
   - d. fuss

8. Beth noticed a moldy substance growing on her feet. She might have concluded that it was a _____.
   - a. funny
   - b. function
   - c. fungus
   - d. fuss

9. Andre's grandmother died. The family must now make _____ arrangements.
   - a. fun
   - b. funeral
   - c. furry
   - d. furor

10. Jason has studied every night for many hours for his math test, but he is worrying too much. It is good that Jason studied, but he is creating too much of a _____ by worrying.
    - a. fuss
    - b. furious
    - c. furor
    - d. fungus

11. In my literature class, we are going to study these three females. Who are these three?
    - a. fungus
    - b. furor
    - c. funeral
    - d. Furies

12. The clown at the circus seemed to be _____ as he limped off stage, yelling angrily about his broken ankle.
    - a. funny
    - b. furor
    - c. fun
    - d. furious

STOP

APPLYING LIBRARY SKILLS
READING A TABLE OF CONTENTS

ACTIVITY: Read the following table of contents from a magazine. Then answer the questions that follow.

CONTENTS

All stories written and drawn by Kevin Johnson

"In the Knick of Time" .... Before the printer came down.
First published in **AHS Literary Journal**, May 1995.
Colored by April Mitchell.

"Front Page Confusion" .... A coup for faith and Micah.
First published in **AHS Literary Journal**, December 1995.
Colored by Paul Moore.

"An Editorial to David Moore" .... Edited by Jacques Snow.

"The Teacher" .... I have something to say and show.
First published in **AHS Literary Journal**, November 1995.
Colored by Eugene Hayes.

"A Fishy Story" .... There is truth in writing.
First published in **AHS Literary Journal**, October 1995.
Colored by Jessica Silvey.

"Casting Away All the Rules" .... What does David know?
First published in **AHS Literary Journal**, September 1995.
Colored by Chantz Bennett.

Cover colored by Faith Dodson
Cover design by Julia Covert and Jeremy Hinds
#00-90866-8854

---

1. Who wrote the stories in the magazine?
   - a. Chantz Bennett
   - b. Kevin Johnson
   - c. Paul Moore
   - d. Julia Covert

2. Who colored the cover for the magazine?
   - a. Kevin Johnson
   - b. April Mitchell
   - c. Eugene Hayes
   - d. Faith Dodson

3. The story "Front Page Confusion" was first published when?
   - a. December 1995
   - b. May 1995
   - c. November 1995
   - d. October 1995

ANSWER KEY

Page 12
1. vacant
2. mended
3. generous
4. mean

Page 13
1. D
2. O
3. F
4. G
5. B
6. L
7. H
8. E
9. S
10. C
11. J
12. Q
13. N
14. A
15. P
16. K
17. T
18. I
19. R
20. M

Page 14
1. piece
2. fined
3. hour
4. by
5. flour
6. threw
7. hear
8. write
9. road
10. great
11. blue
12. deer
13. meet
14. mail
15. aunt

Page 15
1. h
2. r
3. l
4. b
5. e
6. o
7. u
8. j
9. f
10. s
11. a
12. c
13. n
14. t
15. g
16. k
17. v
18. i
19. m
20. d
21. q
22. p

Page 16
1. begin
2. sunny
3. sad
4. winter
5. old
6. late
7. dangerous
8. polite
9. sleeping
10. easy
11. heavy
12. learn
13. white
14. many
15. quit
16. less
17. sharp
18. fix
19. inside
20. melt

Page 17
Suggested answers
A. 1. under
2. quick
3. excuse
4. watch
5. quiet
6. finish
7. right
8. run
9. lady
10. save

B. 1. cool
2. sad
3. frown
4. take
5. bad
6. remember
7. full
8. learn
9. push
10. hot

C. 1. to
2. write
3. road
4. sun
5. week
6. dear
7. knight
8. pair
9. flower
10. wood

Pages 18-19
1. c
2. b
3. a
4. b
5. c
6. d
7. c
8. a
9. c
10. c
11. c
12. b
13. b
14. a
15. b
16. a
17. d
18. b

Page 20
1. Tom
2. apple
3. opera
4. suit
5. Thursday
6. window
7. wheel
8. Brenda
9. horse
10. October

(Answers to 7 below are suggested; may vary.)
1. aren't
2. doesn't
3. I've
4. isn't
5. hasn't
6. I've
7. haven't

Page 21
1. m
2. g
3. r
4. b
5. j
6. d
7. p
8. l
9. a
10. t
11. f
12. k
13. c
14. i
15. s
16. e
17. n
18. q
19. h
20. o

Page 22-23
1. correct
2. shake
3. state
4. very many
5. smart
6. plan
7. skillful
8. silly
9. forecasting

91

10. greatest
11. swap
12. correct
13. expensive
14. angry
15. weak
16. everyday
17. short
18. reckless

Page 24
1. the planet's name
2. 36
3. my furry friends

Page 25
1. Jorge
2. Adam
3. Adam
4. attend college
5. Monica
6. Jorge

Page 26
1. Florida
2. marlin
3. six feet long
4. purple
5. shark
6. in the ocean

Page 27
1. mountain laurel
2. wildflowers
3. time
4. wildflowers

Page 29
1. Queen Isabella
2. Italy
3. *Santa Maria*
4. San Salvador
5. the Indies
6. Spain

Page 30
1. skating
2. on the ice
3. skater

Page 32
1. in a grocery store
2. ran into the door
3. sweat
4. through the automatic door
5. list

Page 33
1. sleep
2. thesaurus
3. musician
4. beautiful
5. fun

Page 34
1. The Bark of a Tree
2. bark
3. outside covering of the tree
4. protect from injury and harm

Page 35
1. white
2. Space Camp
3. in northern Alabama
4. southern
5. National Aeronautics and Space Administration

Page 36
1. Spain
2. dah-lee
3. Surrealism
4. Freud

Page 37
1. Erlanger
2. for himself
3. vacation
4. write the company

Page 38
1. A
2. D

Pages 39-40
A. 1		B. 3		C. 4	
D. 4		E. 2		F. 3	
G. 4		H. 1		I. 3	
J. 1		K. 3		L. 1	
M. 4		N. 2		O. 4	
P. 1		Q. 3		R. 4	
S. 2		T. 4		U. 1	

Page 41
1. careing
2. kamera
3. fryed
4. terkey
5. enjoied
6. playyed
7. meazure
8. pathatic
9. seperated
10. immpressed
11. shakking
12. tenent
13. yelow
14. proffessional

Pages 42-43
1. exercise
2. circle
3. statement
4. it's
5. January
6. business
7. accept
8. Lemonade
9. theirs
10. pair
11. friend
12. opportunity
13. shoulder
14. Patience
15. bought
16. convince
17. quality
18. duty

Page 44
1. the movie how much
2. I cant find the book I
3. thousands of years. the

Page 45
1. ?
2. none
3. ,
4. :

1. may I go with Tom to
2. My aunt lives there she has
3. Seattle Washington last
4. tomorrow" asked Jill. I may

Page 46
1. Huron SD 57350
2. Dear Peggy
3. My class is reading the book I am
4. Love

1. My speech in class yesterday was one of the best I've given.
2. His grandmother lives in St. Cloud, Florida.

Page 47
1. We could see the historic home on Rue Lane Drive.
2. Are you going to the open house, Jonah?
3. "Get out of here!" joked the announcer.

1. The sun shining so warm.
2. Call me in the morning at 600.
3. My friends nickname is Bill
4. No mistakes
5. Dec. 5 1994, from Paris.
6. the bruno's that

Page 48
1. Greece in 776 B.C.
2. Munich, Seoul, and Lake Placid.
3. Atlanta, a
4. southeastern United States.

1. elementary school
2. night. may I give you a
3. a big mac and a large
4. in florida, one of my

Page 49
1. May 29, 1995
2. Dear Cynthia,
3. costume I
4. you. Thank
5. Your friend,

Page 50
1. Now, they is good friends.
2. He don't like to go outside
3. to the most deepest part.
4. No mistakes

Page 51
1. What's for supper tonight?
2. She had driven the car before.
3. Is he smaller than she?
4. Buying the house was lots of fun.
5. Doesn't anybody know?
6. Laughing, they jumped.
7. I hope to meet him.

1. Me and Michael enjoy Salvador
2. Wes' family and us are going

Page 52
1. trees
2. we
3. apples
4. Mercury

5. ran
6. had written
7. are going
8. knew

Page 53
1. C
2. D
3. C

Page 54
1. C

1. A
2. D
3. B

Page 55
1. D
2. A

1. their
2. am having
3. her
4. is wearing

Page 56
1. hotter
2. or
3. smaller
4. has given
5. prettier
6. tallest

1. John and Jason are my best friends.

Page 57
1. My principal, Mr. Finkelstein, has a wife and four children.
2. I have a pet cat, Simon, that is white with one black spot.

1. My grandfather is the greatest man in the world.

Page 58
Topic Sentences:
   I am very proud to attend my school.
Supporting Sentences:
   Sometimes he was not treated kindly and fairly, and once he was put in jail for several days in Birmingham, Alabama.

Page 59
1. He don't ever come to class
2. He has broke the handle in
3. and I was discussing it.
4. No mistakes
5. There is apples and oranges
6. rode three times already.
7. The dog it was my pet
8. I would of gone with you,
9. Jennifer knowed she was
10. Larry he knows how to
11. pen pal lately? I speak to

Pages 60-61
1. 312
2. 298
3. 232
4. 27
5. 48
6. 253
7. 90
8. 224
9. 722
10. 41
11. 25
12. 56
13. 96
14. 2/4
15. 4/8

Page 62
1. N
2. 19
3. 57
4. 279
5. 10
6. 18
7. 97
8. 2800
9. 2040
10. 1566
11. 1806
12. 102

Page 63
1. 258
2. 202
3. 20
4. 50
5. 30
6. 1836
7. 654
8. 1042
9. 909
10. 26
11. 2877
12. 489

Page 64
1. 3024
2. 11200
3. 2298
4. 13
5. 12
6. 12
7. 500
8. N
9. 66
10. 1
11. 41
12. 992

Page 65
1. 56
2. 12
3. 1½
4. 121
5. 318
6. 1554
7. 16
8. 1/12
9. 6110
10. 16
11. 11600
12. 108
13. 28
14. 1/8
15. 48
16. 600

Page 66
1. c
2. a
3. c
4. d
5. d
6. b
7. a
8. d
9. a
10. c
11. d
12. a
13. d
14. c
15. a
16. d
17. c
18. a
19. d
20. b
21. a

Page 67
1. b
2. c
3. c
4. d
5. b
6. c
7. b
8. c
9. c
10. b
11. c
12. a
13. a
14. c
15. d

Pages 68-70
1. 5
2. three thousand two hundred fifty-one
3. b
4. x
5. 9 inches
6. 1241
7. 40
8. 60
9. 216
10. 9
11. 18
12. 36 ÷ 3 + 12
13. $2.51
14. 39
15. 3
16. triangle
17. 2
18. 27
19. 812

Page 71
1. 11
2. ¼
3. 3
4. 90
5. 30 x 2 + 5
6. 150, 153, 156, 159
7. c
8. 6

Page 72
1. Lisa
2. 5
3. 12

Page 73
1. 18
2. June 22
3. 1 quarter + 3 dimes
4. 3
5. $80
6. 6
7. 48
8. $.04

Page 74
1. 5:00
2. 3:00
3. a
4. 93
5. $2.26
6. 1270
7. red

Page 75
1. 100
2. 1200
3. 4
4. 3
5. $200
6. answer not given
7. 200
8. $2.50

Page 76
1. 4
2. 17
3. 13

Page 77
1. 9th
2. 3/6
3. 3
4. 1/4
5. 375
6. 1/5
7. 5

8. $2.67

Page 78
1. 8
2. Malika
3. Jeff
4. Kevin

Page 79
1. Mark
2. Nan
3. 5
4. 27

Page 80
1. c
2. b
3. b
4. c

Page 81
1. b
2. c
3. d
4. b

Page 82
1. c
2. a
3. b
4. a
5. d
6. b

Page 83
1. b
2. c
3. a
4. d
5. b
6. d
7. a

Page 84
1. c
2. d
3. c

Page 86
1. c
2. a
3. c
4. b
5. 212
6. a

Page 87
1. Perth
2. a capital
3. Tasmania
4. northeast
5. Indian Ocean

Page 89
1. c
2. b
3. d
4. b
5. a
6. d
7. c
8. c
9. b
10. a
11. d
12. d

Page 90
1. b
2. d
3. a